SLANG FROM
SHAKESPEARE

SLANG FROM SHAKESPEARE

TOGETHER WITH LITERARY EXPRESSIONS

COMPILED BY
ANDERSON M. BATEN

DOVER PUBLICATIONS
Garden City, New York

This Dover edition, first published in 2023, is an unabridged
republication of the work originally published
by Anderson M. Baten in 1931.

Library of Congress Cataloging-in-Publication Data

Names: Shakespeare, William, 1564–1616. | Baten, Anderson M.
(Anderson Monroe), 1888–1943, compiler.
Title: Slang from Shakespeare : together with literary expressions /
compiled by Anderson M. Baten.
Description: Garden City, New York : Dover Publications, 2023. |
Summary: "This book is a compendium of phrases from
Shakespeare that have been used for hundreds of years. Sections
of the book include epigrams, invectives, poems of philosophy, and
beautiful literary expressions, all of which make Shakespeare such
an enduring and timeless writer"—Provided by publisher.
Identifiers: LCCN 2023016458 | ISBN 9780486852003 (trade
paperback)
Subjects: LCSH: Shakespeare, William, 1564–1616—Quotations. |
English language—Early modern, 1500–1700—Slang. |
Quotations, English. | Figures of speech.
Classification: LCC PR2892 .B37 2023 | DDC 822.3/3—dc23/
eng/20230512
LC record available at https://lccn.loc.gov/2023016458

Manufactured in the United States of America
85200801   2023
www.doverpublications.com

PREFACE

The object of this little book is to call your attention to the fact that there is nothing new under the sun. We still use these phrases from Shakespeare that have been used for hundreds of years.

In the other sections of this book you will find the epigrams, invectives, poems of philosophy and beautiful literary expressions that make Shakespeare stand out as the greatest intellectual prodigy Nature has produced.

As it's been said, "We get knowledge from Shakespeare, not with painful labor, as we dig gold from the mine, but at leisure, and with delight, as we gain health and vigor from the sports of the field."

After you have read the expressions in this book, you will see there is nothing new. One age picks up the habits of the old age and carries them on. These are plagiarists, some say; others say it is the law of human nature. "Today is the pupil of yesterday. Man is an infant born at midnight, who, when he sees the sun rise, thinks that yesterday has never existed."

—ANDERSON M. BATEN

CONTENTS

SLANG FROM SHAKESPEARE

SECTION I

~∂~

SLANG EXPRESSIONS FROM SHAKESPEARE STILL IN USE

A

A box on the ear.
A crow of the same nest.
A feather will turn the scale.
A dish fit for the gods.
A garment out of fashion.
A good man's fortune may grow out at heels.
A hand open as day.
A hare-brained.
A hell of a time.
A horse! a horse! my kingdom for a horse.
A horse of that color.
A lion among ladies.
A man can die but once.
A man is master of his liberty.
A match, sir.
A mile beyond the moon.
A notorious liar.
A pinion of his wing.
A plain blunt man.
A right fair mark.
A sad tale's best for winter.
A truth's a truth.
A very fresh-fish here.
A very man *per se*.
Able to speak for himself.

Above the bounds of reason.
Addle as an egg.
After all this fooling.
Against the grain.
Against the tooth of time.
Almost as like as eggs.
All hail to thee.
All hell shall stir for this.
All is one to him.
All is said.
All is well that ends well.
All men are bad.
All the better.
All the fat is in the fire.
All the world's a stage.
All will come to nought.
An eyesore.
An eye-wink of her.
An itching palm.
An if you break the ice.
And believe it.
And keep their teeth clean.
And not be all day neither.
And so it is.
And thank heaven.
And the old saying is.
And thereby hangs a tale.
And strut in his gait.
And to be plain.
And, upon my life.
And what is her history? A blank.

And what say you to this.
And would to God.
Answer me in one word.
Any thing possible.
Apple of his eye.
Apron men.
Are brim full, our cause is ripe.
Are you a native of this place?
Are you aweary of me?
Are you so hot?
Are you sure of that?
As a cat laps milk.
As a cat to steal cream.
As a fair day in summer.
As a nose on a man's face.
As cold as a dead man's nose.
As cold as any stone.
As far as day does night.
As fat as butter.
As fresh as May.
As gentle as a lamb.
As good a plot as ever was laid.
As good as rotten.
As good luck would have it.
As greatest does least.
As it were.
As it were doomsday.
As jealous as a turkey.
As merry as crickets.
As nail in door.
As poor as Job.

As pure as snow.
As tedious as a twice-told tale.
As tedious as hell.
As the destinies decree.
As they say.
As sure as day.
As sure as his guts are made of puddings.
As water in a sieve.
As you said.
At arm's end.
At last it rains.
At the arm's end.
At the fingers' ends.
At thy elbow.
At your service.
Away, ass.
Ay, on my life.

B

Bad in the best.
Bad turn to worse.
Bait the hook well; this fish will bite.
Bask'd him in the sun.
Be a man.
Be as good as thy word.
Be brief.
Be it known unto all men by these presents.
Be it so.
Be jolly.
Be not so hot.

Be of good cheer.
Be wise.
Be my hen.
Be wise, then.
Be used as you do use your dog.
Bear with me.
Beat him like a dog.
Beat it.
Bed-rid.
Before not dreamt of.
Being dumb.
Believe, I will.
Believe it.
Believe it, this is true.
Believe me.
Believe me, they butt together well.
Better once than never, for never too late.
Better three hours too soon than a minute too late.
Bibble babble.
Birds of self-same feather.
Bite my thumb at them.
Block-head.
Both take and give.
Boys are boys.
Brain him.
Breath of garlic-eaters.
Bring the roof to the foundation.
Bristle thy courage up.
Budge not.
Bugbears.
Bully sir.

But, be it as it may.
But for loving me.
But, hit or miss.
But how.
But how comes.
But I can tell you one thing.
But I know what I know.
But I'll bridle it.
But it sufficeth.
But screw your courage to the sticking place.
But the point is this.
But to answer you as you would be understood.
But to be frank.
But yet.
By and by.
By God.
By God's help.
By Jove.
By Jove I vow.
By St. Paul.
By underhand injustice.
By underhand means.
By word of mouth.

C

Call it by what you will.
Call it what you will.
Call some knight, that hath a stomach.
Can he not be sociable?
Can serve my turn.

Can such things be?
Care killed a cat.
Cashier'd.
Cattle of this color.
Cock-sure.
Cheek by jowl.
Chew upon this.
Chide at him.
Cold as snow-ball.
Comb your noodle.
Come, come.
Come, come, I'll hear no more of this.
Come on.
Come on, come on.
Come what come may.
Confound thee.
Crabbed age.
Crack of doom.
Curd thy blood.
Curse my bones.
Custom hath made it.
Cut one another's throat.
Cut-throat dog.

D

Damn her.
Damn me.
Dead as a door nail.
Dead? As a door nail.
Death is the end of all.

Death will have his day.
Deny if you can.
Devil rides upon a fiddle-stick.
Devoutly dotes.
Die men, like dogs.
Die with harness on our back.
Did it on my free-will.
Disgraces have of late knocked too often at my door.
Do as I advise.
Do as thou wilt.
Do contest as hotly.
Do it on a full stomach.
Do it wisely.
Do it with judgment.
Do it with unwashed hands.
Do not presume too much.
Do not swear at all.
Do you know what you say?
Dog the heels.
Dog will have his day.
Dooms-day.
Doomsday is near.
Done me wrong.
Dote on.
Dote on you.
Dote upon a man.
Dote upon my love.
Dotes on.
Drinking will undo you.
Dry as hay.
Dumb wise men.

E

Ebb and flow.
Elbows him.
Ere you ask, is given.
Even for an egg shell.
Every inch a king.
Every man has his fault.
Exceedingly well read.

F

Faint not faint heart.
Faithful friends are hard to find.
False as dice.
False as hell.
Familiarity will grow more contempt.
Fare thee well.
Fasten your ear on my advisings.
Fat is in the fire.
Fetch in our wood.
Fetch us in fuel.
Fewer words than a parrot.
Fiddlestick.
Fie, fob, and fum, I smell the blood of a Britishman.
Five for one.
Fled like quicksilver.
Foamed at the mouth.
Fold down the leaf where I have left.
Food for powder.
Fool, fool.

Foot ball players.
Foot it.
For, by the way.
For God's sake.
For goodness' sake.
For heaven's sake.
For Jesus Christ.
For Jesus' sake.
For my part.
For pity's sake.
For so much trash.
For the love of God.
For the love of laughter.
For this will out.
For who's so dumb.
For your own sake.
Forget them.
Freeze in my saddle.
Fright the ladies out of their wits.
Fresh as a bridegroom.
From post to pillar.
From stem to stern.
From the crown of his head to the sole of his foot.
From top to toe.

G

Gave me cold looks.
Gave up the ghost.
Gaze your fill.
Get the better of them.

Get you gone.
Give me air.
Give it, or take it.
Give me my sin again.
Give me your hand.
Give me your thoughts.
Given them gratis.
Give the devil his due.
Give thee thy due.
Go at once.
Go fetch it.
Go, get thee hence.
Go hang yourself.
Go hang yourselves all.
Go on.
Go on, go on.
Go rot.
Go shake your ears.
Go tiptoe.
Go to.
Go to, go to.
Go to hell for it.
Go to it.
Go to then.
Go you into hell.
God damn me.
God be with you.
God knows, I will not do it.
God is my witness.
God made him, and therefore let him pass for a man.
God save you.

Good as the best.
Good for nothing.
Good friend.
Good God.
Grant my need.
Grant that, and tell me.
Grates me.
Green-eyed jealousy.
Grounded upon no other argument.

H

Hack our English.
Had I the heart to do it.
Hair-breadth escapes.
Hair to stand on end.
Hang all the husbands.
Hang it.
Hang themselves in their own straps.
Hanging is too good.
Hard-hearted man.
Harp not on that.
Harp not on that string.
Harp on that still.
Harping on what I am.
Has turned almost the wrong side out.
Haste still pays haste.
Hath been a man or two lately killed about her.
Hath been the spoil of me.
Hath his bellyful.
Have a beard grow in the palm of my hand.

Have done a good day's work.
Have mercy on thee.
Have patience.
Have these gifts a curtain before them.
Have worn your eyes almost out in the service.
Have you forgot all sense of place and duty?
Have you no modesty?
Have you the heart?
Havock.
He did love her: But how.
He does me double wrong.
He dreads his wife.
He durst as well.
He foams at mouth.
He hangs the lip at something.
He has where-withal.
He hath a heart as sound as a bell.
He hath done me wrong.
He hath eaten me out of house and home.
He is a cat still.
He is a cat to me.
He is a very dog.
He is about it.
He is an ass.
He is made forever.
He is mewed up.
He is now at a cold scent.
He is of note.
He is out at elbow.
He is out of tune.
He is something peevish.

He is wise.
He knew his man.
He knows the game.
He knows too much.
He looks successfully.
He loves himself.
He makes a July's day short as December.
He raves.
He speaks the common tongue.
He talks at random.
He wants nothing.
He was a man.
He was mad for her.
He will steal himself into a man's favor.
He winks.
He's a bear.
He's moody.
He's the devil.
He's the very devil.
Hear it not.
Heaven knows, not I.
Heigh ho.
Hell is here.
Here comes my man.
Here he comes swelling like a turkey cock.
Here is my hand.
Hey ho.
Hide my bones.
His cares are now all ended.
His ebbs, his flows.
His face I know not.

His face is the worst thing about him.
His knees knocking each other.
Hob, nob.
Hood-wink him.
Hoot him out.
Hope to reap the fame.
Hot as gunpowder.
Hot ice.
How do you know.
How do you mean removing him.
How goes the world.
How goes the world with you.
How green you are.
How he coasts.
How I dote on thee.
How imagination blows him.
How is it with you.
How is that.
How my bones ache.
How say you.
How say you to that.
How the world goes.
How the world wags.
How to cheat the devil.
How well he's read.
How you do talk.

I

I am a bunch of radish.
I am a man.

I am a woman's man.
I am almost out at heels.
I am amaz'd, and know not what to say.
I am an ass.
I am as hot as molten lead, as heavy too.
I am as poor as Job.
I am damned in hell.
I am dumb.
I am firm.
I am in your debt.
I am made an ass.
I am not of that feather.
I am on fire.
I am sick when I do look on thee.
I am that I am.
I am the mistress.
I am too sure of it.
I am as ugly as a bear.
I am very ill at ease.
I am well spoken of.
I am your shadow.
I, an old turtle.
I beseech you.
I can cut a caper.
I can cut the mutton, to it.
I can go no further.
I can give you inkling.
I can hardly believe that.
I can swim like a duck.
I cannot rid my hands of him.
I cannot tell what the dickens his name is.

I could brain him.
I could never say grace.
I crave your honor's pardon.
I do adore thee.
I do not call your faith in question.
I do not like this fooling.
I dote.
I dote on his very absence.
I did dote.
I did dote upon.
I did upbraid her.
I discard you.
I durst go no further.
I durst not speak.
I fear no bugbears.
I feel it upon my bones.
I freely speak my mind.
I had rather be a beggar's dog.
I had rather be a dog.
I had rather be a dog and bay the moon.
I have been in such a pickle.
I have dogged him.
I have heard it all.
I have him between my finger and my thumb.
I have lost my teeth in your service.
I have lost myself.
I have my belly full.
I have no ears to his request.
I have not deserved this.
I have not sounded him.
I have not the face to say.

I have o'ershot myself.

I have seen better faces in my time.

I have reason good enough.

I have spoke the truth.

I have spoke to the purpose.

I have taken you napping.

I have thee on the hip.

I have them at my fingers' ends.

I hope all's for the best.

I hope I have your good will.

I hope so.

I hope to frame thee.

I knew you at the first.

I know a trick worth two of that.

I know him.

I know him a notorious liar.

I know his gait.

I know my place.

I know my price.

I know you of old.

I marvel how he sped.

I may do that I shall be sorry of.

I might rail at him.

I mind to tell him plainly what I think.

I must be patient.

I must confess.

I must hold my tongue.

I must serve my turn.

I need not add more fuel to your fire.

I never saw the like.

I never stood on ceremonies.

I pant for life.
I pause for a reply.
I play the devil.
I play'd the fool.
I promised to eat all of his killing.
I remember you by the sound of your voice.
I saw her first.
I saw his heart in his face.
I shall be pinched to death.
I shall forget myself.
I shall laugh myself to death.
I shall not be slack.
I should die with laughing.
I smell a device.
I smell false Latin.
I smell it.
I stood like a man at a mark.
I take it.
I thank God I am not a woman.
I thank my stars I am happy.
I think thou art an ass.
I thought all for the best.
I told her so.
I told you so.
I told you what would come of this.
I utterly abhor, yea, from my soul.
I was too hot.
I weep for joy.
I weigh it lightly.
I will be as good as my word.
I will make a lip.

I will make him dance.

I will never trust his word.

I will not bait thee.

I will not budge a foot.

I will put it in practice.

I will speak daggers to her.

I will supplant some of your teeth.

I will tell him a little piece of my desire.

I will tell him my mind.

I will venture.

I will wink.

I would crave a word or two.

I would I knew his mind.

I would not be in some of your coats.

I would not for a million.

I would not have given it for a wilderness of
    monkeys.

I would not have you forget yourself.

I would to God.

I would to heaven.

I would to heaven, he were.

If he could right himself.

If he fall in, good night.

If it might not be presumption.

If justice had her right.

If love be blind.

If a man's brains were in his heels.

If not, why, so.

If she lives till doomsday.

If this fellow be wise.

If you have a stomach to it.

If you say so.
Ill blows the wind that profits nobody.
I'll be as good as my word.
I'll be hanged.
I'll fetch her.
I'll follow you at heels.
I'll hammer it out.
I'll meddle nor make no more in the matter.
I'll never look you in the face.
I'll never put my finger in the fire.
I'll not meddle in it.
I'll pine away.
I'll play the eavesdropper.
I'll not budge an inch.
I'll not stay a jot longer.
I'll see thee hanged first.
I'll set my teeth.
I'll strike home.
I'll tear her all to pieces.
I'll want thee.
In a minute there are many days.
In life's uncertain voyage.
In lieu whereof.
In my mind's eye.
In spite at him.
In spite of spite.
In spite of us.
In the name of heaven.
In the name of truth.
In the twinkling of an eye.
In your dumps.

Indirectly, and directly too.
Is beaten black and blue.
Is dirt to him.
Is he so much?
Is it come to that?
Is it come to this?
Is it not a wise course?
Is it possible?
Is not catching.
Is she so hot.
Is the better man of the two.
Is there no respect in you?
Is this the man you speak of?
Is this well spoken?
It goes much against my stomach.
It grows something stale with me.
It holds current.
It is pity he is not honest.
It is against the rule of nature.
It is all one to me.
It is as easy as lying.
It is better said than done.
It is but quid for quo.
It is but so so.
It is but trash.
It is high time.
It is my duty.
It is my familiar sin.
It is neither here nor there.
It is no less.
It is no other.

It is not my consent.
It is not my fault.
It is not the first time.
It is not worth the feeding.
It is one of those old tricks.
It is pity.
It is pity she's not honest.
It is too hard a knot for me to untie.
It is very much lamented.
It is well said.
It's four to one.
It's not so good.
It makes us, or it mars us.
It nips me.
It serves my purpose.
It serves you well.
It was Greek to me.
It was the death of him.
It were all one.
It would be double dealing.

J

Jack hath no Jill.
Judge you as you are.

K

Keep him above deck.
Keep him out of my sight.
Keep it, I cannot eat it.

Keep on the windy side of the law.
Kill one another by the look.
Knock thy brains out.
Knock too often at my door.
Know him by his gait.
Knowing him is enough.

L

Lay my bones there.
Leap all civil bounds.
Leave not out a jot.
Leaves nothing undone.
Leaving no tract behind.
Led by the nose.
Lest the bargain should catch cold, and starve.
Let her be as she is.
Let it serve for table-talk.
Let me alone.
Let me ask you a question.
Let me feel your pulse.
Let me see.
Let me see, let me see.
Let no dog bark.
Let that go.
Let that suffice you.
Let the ladies tattle what they please.
Let the matter slip.
Let the world slide.
Let them take it as they list.

Let this be granted.
Let us be keen.
Let us make head.
Let us talk in good earnest.
Let worse follow worse.
Let's fight it out.
Let's go hand in hand.
Let's have no more fooling about it.
Lie at my mercy.
Life's uncertain voyage.
Like a cur.
Like a parrot.
Like a prophet.
Like a rat without a tail.
Like a summer's cloud.
Like a thunderbolt.
Like a whale.
Like lesser lights.
Like wild fire.
Logger-head.
Look, here he comes.
Look him in the face.
Look me in the face.
Look, who comes here.
Long live the king.
Lord have mercy on them.
Love all, trust a few.
Love is blind.
Love is my sin.
Loves to hear himself talk.

M

Mad as a March hare.
Made an oyster of me.
Made my eyes water.
Make him cry O.
Make me dote.
Make mouths upon when I turn my back.
Man is but an ass.
Many sharp reasons to defeat the law.
Mark what I say.
Mark you now.
Married to your good service.
May grow out heels.
Men of few words.
Mend your speech a little.
Men's mouths are full of it.
Mere prattle.
Methinks I hear him now.
Mine honor on my promise.
More at your request.
More homely.
More than words can witness.
More than you can dream.
Most unkindest cut of all.
Mouth full of news.
Mouth so watered.
Mum then, and no more.
Must answer for your raising.
Must I budge.

My better parts.
My bird.
My cake is dough.
My cousin meant well.
My finger itches.
My fingers itch.
My friends were poor, but honest.
My hair doth stand on end.
My hazards.
My heart bleeds.
My heart into my mouth.
My heart is turned to stone.
My honor on my promise.
My man is as true as steel.
My mind is changed.
My mind's not on it.
My name be blotted from the book of life.
My nose itches for news.
My old bones ache.
My pride fell with my fortune.
My project gather to a head.
My reputation is at stake.
My reputation stained.
My ships come home.
My soul hath elbow-room.
My wife's a hobbyhorse.
My wife's as jealous as a turkey.
My wife is slippery.
My woman.

N

Napes of your necks.

Needs no excuse.

Net spread for her.

Never knew what truth meant.

New-fangled ill.

New-fangled shows.

Nips youth in the head.

No boy's play here.

No matter.

No more brain than I have in mine elbow.

No more than a fish loves water.

No more of that.

No, nor no where else.

No remedy.

None else.

Not a jot the other.

Not a hair amiss.

Not a mouse stirring.

Not a word.

Not a whit.

Not I, believe me.

Not so hot.

Not till a hot January.

Not the ill wind which blows none too good.

Not too hot.

Nothing else.

Nothing to be got now-a-days, unless canst fish for it.

Not worth a gooseberry.

Not worth an egg.

Nothing becomes him.
Nothing will come of nothing.
Now have I done a good day's work.
Now I come to it.
Now or never, sister.
Now, the devil.
Now the time is flush.

O

O boy.
O devil.
O God.
O, hell.
O it is fair play.
O Jephthah.
O me.
O, my heart bleeds.
O! my word.
O not today.
O pardon me.
O, that I were a man.
O these men, these men.
Of one that loved not wisely, but too well.
Old boy.
Old goat.
Omit not anything.
On my honor.
On my life.
On my word.
One bear will not bite another.

One for all, or all for one.
One of your nine lives.
One single word.
One to ten.
One word.
One word more.
Onion-eyed.
Our cake's dough.
Our day of doom.
Our house is hell.
Our legions are brim-full, our cause is ripe.
Out of my sight.
Out of the jaws of death.
Out of their wits.
Out, scab.
Out-stare him.

P

Pathetical nit.
Peevish boy.
Pick his teeth.
Pinch us black and blue.
Pitchers have ears.
Playing the mouse, in absence of the cat.
Plucked in the bud.
Poor bird.
Poor chicken.
Poor hen.
Poor but honest.

Poor man.
Poor monkey.
Poor rats.
Poor wench.
Poor worm.
Prawls, and prabbles.
Press not a falling man too far.
Pribbles and prabbles.
Prick not your finger.
Pride went before, ambition follows him.
Put me to it.

Q

Quiet as a lamb.
Quips and thy quiddities.

R

Ready to give up the ghost.
Rehearse that once more.
Rest on my word.
Rid the house of her.
Rids his hands of her.
Right as snow in harvest.
Rotten at the heart.
Rotten opinion.
Rotten policy.
Rotten times.
Rumor's tongue.

S

Say but the word.
Say so.
Say that again.
Say what you will.
Say your mind to him.
Says he.
Scratch my head.
Seal up your lips, and give no words but—Mum.
See the coast cleared.
Seek the lion in his den.
Seems to dote on me.
Second to none.
Self-charity be sometimes a vice.
Serve my turn.
Serve your turn.
Set my teeth on edge.
Seven years' heat.
Shake thy bones.
Shall all be done by the rule.
Shall dog them at the heels.
Shall I speak a word in your ear?
Shall take note of him.
She chats him.
She goes off and on at pleasure.
She falls for it.
She failed me once.
She is keen.
She is mine own.
She is my goods.

She is my prize.
She is not hot.
She is peevish.
She is so hot.
She knew her distance.
She spit in his face.
She would run mad for this man.
She's a good wench.
She's lost, past all cure.
She's married not unto my clothes.
She's too rough for me.
Shift a shirt.
Shivered like an egg.
Should catch cold, and starve.
Show it a fair pair of heels.
Shut up.
Sickness is catching.
Silly jeering idiots.
Sip on a cup.
Sit fast.
Skimble-skamble stuff.
Slaying is the word; it is a deed in fashion.
So, so.
So help me God.
So I heard you say.
So much for that.
So said, so done.
So woebegone.
Sol.
Something is rotten in the state of Denmark.
Snail-slow in profit.

Snatch words from my tongue.
Snorting like a horse.
Spare not for cost.
Spark of life be yet remaining.
Speak my mind of him.
Speak freely what you think.
Speak in English.
Speak it in French.
Speak plain and to the purpose.
Speak thy mind.
Speak to the mariners.
Spit at him.
Spite of hell.
Spread yourselves.
Spoke behind your back.
Such a silly.
Such things have been done.
So, get thee gone.
So help me God.
So I heard you say.
So long.
So much for that.
Stalks up and down like a peacock.
Stand by.
Stand upon a slippery place.
Stands without blemish.
Stay a little while.
Stay by me.
Step out of these dumps.
Strike home.
Such an ass.

Such as it is.
Sugared words.
Surely as your feet hit the ground.
Swifter than wind upon a field of corn.
Swim like a duck.

T

Take a homely man's advice.
Take it in what sense thou wilt.
Take no note of him.
Take no note of it.
Take note.
Take pains; be perfect.
Take the hint.
Take you at your word.
Take you down a button-hole lower.
Talk till doomsday.
Talkers are no good doers.
Tears do not become a man.
Tedious as a twice-told tale.
Tell a lie and swear it.
Tell o'er thy tale again.
Tell the tale over.
Tell the truth and shame the devil.
Ten to one.
That house is dark? As hell.
That is my business.
That it should come to this.
That kills my heart.
That wants breathing too.

That was but his fancy, blame him not.
That was well fished for.
That we did, we did for the best.
That young start-up.
That's all.
That's a fault that water will mend.
That's as much as to say.
That's neither here nor there.
That's not my fault.
That's not so.
That's strange.
That's true enough.
That's well said.
That's well spoke.
The author's drift.
The better foot before.
The cat is in the well, ding, dong, bell.
The cat will mew, and the dog will have his day.
The devil can cite Scripture.
The door is open, there lies your way.
The duke was dumb.
The end crowns all.
The face, that map.
The fashion of the time is changed.
The fresh fish.
The hen.
The lesson is but plain.
The livelong day.
The man in the moon.
The man's undone for ever.
The milk of human kindness.

The most opportune place.
The naked truth of it is.
The old cock.
The pig.
The short and the long is.
The sooner the better.
The strangeness of this business.
The tender nibbler would not touch the bait.
The time has been.
The time, the place.
The under-world.
The weakest goes to the wall.
The word is over-worn.
Then, as I said.
Then come what can come.
Then to the point.
There be nothing new.
Thereby hangs a tale.
There is nothing new.
There is a thing within my bosom tells me.
There is no time for all things.
There is some grudge between them.
There is some sap in this.
There is something in the wind.
There may be in the cup a spider steeped.
There's a time for all things.
There's hope in it yet.
There's little can be said.
There's no more to be said.
There's one thing wanting.
There's the humor of it.

There's the point.
There's the short and the long.
There's small choice in rotten apples.
There's something tells me.
There's vinegar and pepper in it.
These things are beyond us all.
They are at it.
They butt together well.
They durst not do it.
They go like lightning.
They have all been touched.
They have had inkling.
They know not what they do.
They look like drowned mice.
They never learned that of me.
They prick'd their ears.
They say.
They were red-hot.
They will steal anything.
They will take no offence.
Think on it.
Think on this.
Thinks himself a better man than I am.
This admits no excuse.
This coming summer.
This has been some behind-door work.
This house is turned upside down.
This is a cold beginning.
This is a fellow of the selfsame color.
This is all.
This is as you say.

This is desperate.

This is stiff news.

This is the short and long of it.

This is the silliest stuff that ever I heard.

This is the sum of all.

This is the worst.

This is to make an ass of me.

This spark will prove a raging fire.

This tiger-footed rage.

This will out.

This woman's an easy glove.

Those baby eyes.

Thou art a very ragged wart.

Thou art all ice.

Thou art made.

Thou art pinched for it now.

Thou hast hit it.

Thou hast misconstrued every thing.

Though 't is my familiar sin.

Thrust those down his throat.

Thy eyes shall be thy judge.

Thy case shall be my precedent.

Thy kindness freezes.

Thy love is worth a million.

Tiddie taddle.

Till doomsday.

Tittle-tattling.

To be brief.

To bait me.

To be a spokesman.

To be my henchman.

To be rid of it.

To beg your pardon.

To cudgel you.

To go tiptoe.

To ease my mind.

To eye him.

To hell.

To make him an example.

To pass away the time.

To please the palate of my appetite.

To pry into.

To put in practice.

To put it in execution.

To put you to it.

To right your wrongs.

To square yourself.

To step out of these sudden dumps.

To strut before.

To the quick.

To the last man.

Too good to be so.

Too headstrong for their mother.

Too hot, too hot.

Too late.

Too much of a good thing.

Too spruce, too affected, too odd.

Topsy-turvy.

Trifles, light as air.

True as steel.

True love never did run smooth.

Trust none; for oaths are straws.

Truth will out.
Truth loves open dealing.
Truth will come to light.
Turned the wrong side out.
Tush.
Tush, tush.
Tut.
Tut, man.
Tut, tut.
Twenty to one.
Two may keep counsel.

U

Uneasy lies the head that wears a crown.
Underwrit.
Unkindness strikes a deeper wound than steel.
Until my eyelids will no longer wag.
Up in the air.
Up to the ears.
Upon a homely object.
Upon my life.

V

Venge this wrong.
Very well.

W

Wall-eyed.
Was for my service born.

Waspish-headed.
Watch the clock.
Watch your safety.
Water cannot wash away your sin.
We are all made.
We are all undone.
We are lucky, boy.
We are no tell-tales.
We are women's men.
We burn daylight.
We have kissed away.
We have seen better days.
We know your drift.
We must not make a scarecrow of the law.
We put a sting in him.
We shall be dogged with company.
We sit too long on trifles.
We speak not what we mean.
We stand upon our manners.
We understand not one another.
We were born to die.
We will be short with you.
We will fall for it.
We will not move a foot.
Well come what will.
Well, go to.
Well, go your way.
Well met.
Well said.
Well spoken.
Well taken.

Well; what further.
Well worth the seeing.
We'll do anything for gold.
We'll fight it out.
We'll outface them, and outswear them too.
We'll teach you.
What an ass am I.
What an ass art thou.
What an ass it is.
What a block art thou.
What a blunt fellow.
What a case am I in.
What a fool am I.
What a pied ninny.
What a wasp-tongue.
What do you think me?
What fire is in mine ears.
What hast thou done?
What have I done?
What I can do, can do no hurt to try.
What is done cannot be now amended.
What is it o'clock?
What is that to him?
What is the matter, sweetheart?
What is the news?
What is the time of day?
What must be shall be.
What news on the Rialto?
What news with you?
What of that?
What say you?

What say'st thou?
What say'st thou to this?
What shall thou expect?
What the devil.
What the devil art thou?
What time a day is it?
What you will command me, will I do.
What was it to you?
What's done cannot be undone.
What's done is done.
What's his name?
What's in a name?
What's mine is yours, and what is yours is mine.
What's that to thee?
What's that to us?
What's the matter?
What's the news?
What's the news with you?
What's your will?
When time is ripe.
When you find him out you have him ever after.
Where did I leave?
Where's my man?
Which gives men stomach to digest his words.
While it is hot I'll put it to the issue.
While the grass grows.
Whip the devil around the stump.
Who can find the bent of woman's fancy?
Who ever saw the like?
Who is it can read a woman?
Who picked my pocket?

Who the devil.
Who will believe thee?
Whose fault is this?
Whose sole name blisters our tongue.
Why, a horse can do no more.
Why ask you this?
Why man.
Why, so can I.
Why stay we to be baited?
Why, that's nothing.
Why, what's that to you?
Wild as young bulls.
Wind up my watch.
Wink again.
Wild-goose chase.
Will go your way.
Will shoot point-blank.
Will he stand to it.
Will never out of my bones.
Will not bear question.
Will rail against.
Will undo us all.
Will you take eggs for money?
Will you vouchsafe me?
Will you woo this wild cat?
Wishing him my meat.
Wisely was it said.
With all my heart.
With an eye of green in it.
With halters on their necks.
With his horn full of good news.

Wilt thou be dumb?
Wink at me, and say thou saw'st me not.
Wink each at other.
Wisely too fair.
Wisely was it said.
Words are too precious to be cast away.
Worse than hell.
Worth six of them.
Would be even with her.
Would hang us every mother's son.
Would I were dead.
Would it were otherwise.
Would thou had'st never been born.
Would you imagine.
Would you were half so honest.
Would you?

Y

Ye are all dunces.
Ye gods.
Yet I am not altogether an ass.
You are an ass.
You are a dog.
You are a fool.
You are cold.
You are my man.
You are too cold.
You are not worth the dust which the rude wind
    blows in your face.
You are too hard for me.

You are too hot.
You are very short with us.
You are waspish.
You broke your word.
You can do better yet.
You cat.
You cram these words into mine ears.
You cur.
You do me wrong.
You dog.
You cannot tell who's your friend.
You dote on her.
You had a motive for it.
You egg.
You have broken the article of your oath.
You have done me wrong.
You have hit the mark.
You have laid your heads together.
You have too much respect.
You have your hands full.
You take me in too dolorous a sense.
You keep on the windy side.
You kiss by the book.
You know me.
You know me by my habit.
You know my price.
You look as you had something more to say.
You need not stop your nose.
You may as well say.
You may go so far.
You may ride us.

You must have the patience to hear it.
You must not look so sour.
You old dog.
You polecat.
You rat catcher.
You rogue.
You'll be laughed at.
You'll know more of that hereafter.
You'll lie, like dogs.
You'll mar all.
Your hazard shall be made.

SECTION II

BEAUTIFUL LITERARY EXPRESSIONS

A

A beggar's book out-worths a noble's blood.

A bond of air, strong as the axletree on which heaven rides.

A choice hour.

A figure of truth, of faith, of loyalty.

A finder of occasions.

A gentleman of the very first house.

A little body with a mighty heart.

A lily prison'd in a gaol of snow.

A love that makes breath poor, and speech unable.

A lover's eyes will gaze an eagle blind.

A mountain of mummy.

A rare engineer.

A rarer spirit never did stir humanity.

A spur to valiant and magnanimous deeds.

A table full of welcome.

A throne where honor may be crown'd.

A volume of farewells.

A whole school of tongues.

Alabaster innocent arms.

All grace be in one woman.

All his mind is bent to holiness.

All places that the eye of heaven visits.

All seeing heaven.

All seeing sun.

All springs reduce their currents to mine eyes.
All thy letters suns.
All-too-precious you.
Ambition cannot pierce a wink beyond.
Ambitious past all thinking.
Amorous looking-glass.
And fame, in time to come, canonize us.
And given grace a double majesty.
And, like a mountain cedar, reach his branches to all
    the plains about him.
And sounded all the depths and shoals of honor.
Age, nor honor, shall shape privilege.
Angel-like perfection.
Anointed deputies of heaven.
Audacious without impendency.
As a wren's eye.
As broad and general as the casing air.
As chaste as is the bud ere it be blown.
As chaste as unsunn'd snow.
As clear as in the summer's sun.
As easy as a down-bed.
As full of spirit as the month of May.
As infants empty of all thought.
As iron to adamant, as earth to the center.
As long as heaven, and nature, lengthens it.
As many farewells as be stars in heaven.
As patient as the midnight sleep.
As pearls from diamonds dropp'd.
As rich with praise as is the ooze and bottom of the
    sea.
As secure as sleep.

As sun to day, as turtle to her mate.

As swift as lead.

As true as steel, as plantage to the moon.

As true as truth's simplicity.

As valiant as the wrathful dove, or most magnanimous mouse.

As water is in water.

B

Base men by his endowment are made great.

Bearing the badge of faith.

Beyond the mark of thought.

Blushing discontented sun.

Book of words.

Brow of justice.

C

Cables of perdurable toughness.

Can make vile things precious.

Celestial sun.

Certain stars shot madly from their spheres.

Chaste and immaculate in very thought.

Chaste as ice, as pure as snow.

Chaste as the icicle.

Chaste eye.

Clad with wisdom's majesty.

Cherubim look.

Chop-logic.

Cloud of dignity.

Coin heaven's image.
Commander of my thoughts.
Confirmed honesty.
Conjures the wandering stars, and makes them
    stand.
Consideration like an angel came.
Cool reason.
Courageous captain of compliments.
Crystal looks.
Cutting the clouds.

D

Darts his light through every guilty hole.
Dearer than eyesight, space, and liberty.
Devoted and heart-burning heat of duty.

E

Eagle-sighted eye.
Eagle-winged pride.
Effects of courtesy, dues of gratitude.
Everlasting love.
Even to the utmost syllable of your worthiness.

F

Fairer than tongue can name thee.
Fame's eternal date, for virtue's praise.
Famous memory.
Faster than springtime showers comes thought on
    thought.

Fee simple of my life.
Fights by the book of arithmetic.
Figures pedantical.
Flower of courtesy.
Flowery tenderness.
From Cupid's shoulder pluck his painted wings.
Fortune brings in some boats that are not steer'd.
Free as mountain winds.

G

General all-ending day.
Gilded butterflies.
Give audience to any tongue, speak it of what it will.
Give me a staff of honor for mine age.
Golden multitudes.
Good morrow—ay, and good next day too.
Grace in all simplicity.

H

Hang up philosophy.
Have at you with a proverb.
Have taken treasure from her lips.
Having the truth of honor in her.
Here comes the almanack of my true date.
Heavenly moisture, air of grace.
Heaven's breath.
Heaven's vault.
He cares not, he'll obey conditions.
He cut our roots in character.
He is as full of valor as of kindness.

He is full of harmony.

He is the card or calendar of gentry.

He leads himself.

He throws without distinction.

He was not born to shame.

Hercules himself must yield to odds.

He's walked the way of nature.

He's winding up the watch of his wit; by and by it will
   strike.

Her azure veins, her alabaster skin.

Her bed is India; there she lies, a pearl.

Her coral lips, her snow white dimpled chin.

Her eyelids, cases to those heavenly jewels, begin to
   part their fringes of bright gold.

Her hand, in whose comparison all whites are ink.

Her looks do argue her replete with modesty.

High-judging Jove.

High sparks of honor.

His deeds exceed all speech.

His dews fall everywhere.

His eye ambitious, his gait majestical.

His humor is lofty.

His looks are my soul's food.

His own opinion was his law.

His word is more than the miraculous harp.

Honor and lordship are my titles.

Household harmony.

I

I am no great Nebuchadnezzar, not much skill in grass.

I am too much in the sun.

I am your accessory.

I come hither arm'd against myself.

I find she names my very deed of love.

I have no skill in sense to make distinction.

I love thee infinitely.

I love you more than word can wield the matter.

I see it feelingly.

I see virtue in his looks.

I shall now put you to the height of your breeding.

I will believe you by the syllable.

I will run as far as God has any ground.

I'll be as patient as a gentle stream.

I'll come after you, for I cannot go before.

I'll seek him deeper than ever plummet sounded.

I'll take that winter from your lips, fair lady.

I'll take thy word for faith, not ask thine oath.

I'd throw it down for your deliverance as frankly as a pin.

If he be a married man, he is his wife's head.

If honor may be shrouded in a hearse.

Imperial tongue.

In faith, honest, as the skin between his brows.

In her strong toil of grace.

In so high a style, that no man living shall come over it.

In states unborn, and accents yet unknown.

In the world's volume.

In thy face I see the map of honor, truth, and loyalty.

It lies as coldly in him as fire in a flint, which will not show without knocking.

It is her breathing that perfumes the chamber thus.

It is past the infinite of thought.

It is some meteor that the sun exhales.

It is the very riches of thyself.

It will be pastime passing excellent.
Ivory in an alabaster band.

K

Keep your name living to time.
King of smiles.
Knit our powers to the arm of peace.

L

Let her be a principality.
Lights that do mislead the morn.
Like a great sea mark, standing every flaw.
Like a king, and show my sail of greatness.
Like a taper in some monument.
Like glistening Phaeton.
Like patience on a monument.
Like to the glorious sun's transparent beams.
Like wrinkled pebbles in a glassy stream.
Lived by looking on his image.

M

Made him my book.
Make me tongue-tied, speaking of your fame.
Make the rope of his destiny our cable.
Making you ever better than his praise.
Manhood lies upon his tongue.
Manly marrow.

Meet the time as it seeks us.
Mercy breathe within your lips.
Mint of phrases in his brain.
Mine honesty shall be my dower.
Modest as Justice.
Modest as morning.
Mortgaged to thy will.
Monstrous simplicity.
Most radiant, exquisite, and unmatchable beauty.
Mountain of affection.
My counsel is my shield.
My crown is called content.
My crown is in my heart, not on my head.
My duty cannot be silent when I think your highness
    wronged.
My love's more ponderous than my tongue.
My mind exceeds the compass of her wheel.
My mouth shall be thy parliament.
My project gather to a head.
Music from the spheres.
Must wear the print of his remembrance out.

N

Natural graces that extinguish art.
Nature brought him to the door of death.
Never-dying honor.
No tongue could ever pronounce dishonor on her.
No unchaste action or dishonor'd step.
Numbering sands, and drinking oceans dry.

O

O single-soled jist, solely singular for the singleness.
O that I had a title good enough to keep his name
   company.
On Helen's cheek all art of beauty set.
One general tongue unto us.
One that excels the quirks of blazoning pens.
Outgoes the very heart of kindness.
Outran my purpose.
Outrun the heavens.
Outstare the lightning.

P

Painted rhetoric.
Pale as lead.
Passed all expressing.
Passing through nature to eternity.
Patience, is that letter.
Pattern of all patience.
Pendulous air.
Perpetual durance.
Perpetual honor.
Perfumed chambers of the great.
Pity was all the fault that was in me.
Pleasant without scurrility.
Plucks comfort from his looks.
Plural faith.
Potential love.
Princely courtesy.

Profound simplicity.
Promethean heat.
Prosperity be thy page.
Pure heart's truth.

Q

Quenched in the chaste beams of the watery moon.
Quick is mine ear to hear good towards him.

R

Rather the herb of grace.
Regal thoughts.
Replenished sweet work of nature.
Richer than sea and land.
Right royal sovereign.
Rotundity of the world.
Rubies unparagoned.

S

Seal of bliss.
See a wren hawk at a fly.
She is a theme of honor and renown.
She is herself a dowry.
She is too bright to be looked against.
She's all beauty extant, matchless beauty.
Shot through the ear with a love-song.
Show thy descent by gazing against the sun.
Shunless destiny.

Simpler than the infancy of truth.
Skill-less as unpractised infancy.
Smooth as monumental alabaster.
Smooth as oil, soft as young down.
So excellent a touch of modesty.
So he be with me, by him, like a shadow.
Sole monarch of the universal earth.
Sound the bottom of the after-times.
Sovereign grace.
Speak frankly as the wind.
Star-like rise.
Stepping over the bounds of modesty.
Steps me a little higher than his vow.
Strain courtesy.
Strange without heresy.
Strong as a tower in hope.
Strong enough to laugh at misery.
Stubborn-chaste.
Sweet, above thought I love thee.
Sweet cell of virtue and nobility.
Sweet mercy is nobility's true badge.
Sweet smoke of rhetoric.
Sweeten my imagination.
Sweeter than perfume itself.
Sumptuously re-edified.
Sun-like majesty.
Suns of glory.

T

Taffeta phrases, silken terms precise.
Tamer than sleep, fonder than ignorance.

That is a day longer than a wonder lasts.
That love which virtue begs and virtue grants.
That makes the stream seem flowers; thou, oh, jewel.
That young Mars of men.
The appetite of her eye did seem to scorch me.
The book of his good acts.
The bow is bent and drawn, make from the shaft.
The clouds, methought, would open and show riches.
The destinies do cut his thread of life.
The elephant hath joints, but none for courtesy.
The epithets are sweetly varied.
The eye of majesty.
The master-cord of his heart.
The mirror of all courtesy.
The nonpareil of beauty.
The nurse of judgment.
The rude sea grew civil at her song.
The senate-house of planets all die! sit, to knit in her
    their best perfections.
The top of judgment.
The weight of a hair will turn the scales.
The word is well cull'd, chose; sweet and apt.
The words of Mercury are harsh after the songs of
    Apollo.
The virtue of your name.
The very pink of courtesy.
The world is but a word.
The world's large spaces cannot parallel.
Theme of honor's tongue.
There's no time for a man to recover his hair.
They are as innocent as grace itself.
They are set here for examples.

They do discharge their shot of courtesy.

Thine eye would emulate the diamond.

This all-changing world.

This secret is so weighty, it will require a strong faith
to conceal it.

Those heaven-moving pearls.

Thou art a perpetual triumph, an everlasting
bonfire-light.

Thou art e'en as just a man as e'er my conversation
coped withal.

Thou art framed of the firm truth of valor.

Thou art the armorer of my heart.

Thou hast mettle enough in thee to kill care.

Thou pigeon-egg of discretion.

Thou outruns't grace.

Three-pil'd hyperboles, spruce affectation.

Thunder-darter of Olympus.

Thus ready for the way of life or death I wait the
sharpest blow.

Thy eyes' windows fall.

Thy mind is a very opal.

Thy truth then be thy dower.

Tied with the bonds of heaven.

Title in your brain.

To be slow in words is a woman's only virtue.

To inlay heaven with stars.

To thee no star be dark.

Too ceremonious and traditional.

Tongue-tied simplicity.

Tongueless caverns of the earth.

Tongues of heaven.
Tractable to any honest reason.
True-hearted friends.
True nobility.
True-sweet beauty liv'd and died with him.
Truer than truth itself.
Truth hath a quiet breast.
Truth hath better deeds than words to grace.
Twinkling star.
Two-fold vigor.

U

Unborn times.
Unmatchable courage.
Unpublished virtues.
Untainted virtue.
Up in the air, crowned with the golden sun.
Upon his brow shame is ashamed to sit.
Use your brothers brotherly.

V

Valiant as the lion, churlish as the bear, slow as the
    elephant.
Valiant, wise, remorseful, well accomplished.
Very soul of bounty.
Virtues infinite.
Virtuous sin.

W

Weaker than a woman's tear.

Weeping water.

What fine chisel could ever yet cut breath.

When he speaks, the air, a chartered libertine, is still.

When right with right wars who shall be most right?

When tongues speak sweetly, then they name her
    name.

Whose beauty did astonish the survey of richest eyes.

Whose nature is so far from doing harm.

Whose wisdom was a mirror to the wisest.

Which flashes now a phoenix.

Which sounded like a cannon in a vault.

Wide world's revenue.

With frank and with uncurbed plainness.

With your theme, I could overmount the lark.

Witty without affection.

Words are strokes.

Words of sovereignty.

World's large tongue.

World's whole strength into one great arm.

Would dizzy the arithmetic of memory.

Would I were as deep under the earth as I am above.

Y

Yonder in the sun, practising behavior to his own
    shadow.

You are in the state of grace.

You are full of heavenly stuff, and bear the inventory
of your best graces in your mind.

You are your art's master.

You fur your gloves with reason.

You have a vice of mercy in you.

You have spoken truer than you purposed.

You have the grace of God, sir, and he hath enough.

You know the very road into his kindness.

You taught me how to know the face of right.

You would sound me from my lowest note to the top
of my compass.

Your eyes are lode-stars, and your tongue's sweet air.

Your grace has given a precedent of wisdom.

Your reasons have been sharp and sententious.

Your worth, wide as the ocean.

SECTION III

INVECTIVES

A

A brittle glory shineth in his face.

A curse begin at every root of his heart.

A damned saint, an honorable villain.

A disease, that must be cut away.

A giant traitor.

A greedy ear.

A long-tongued babbling gossip.

A nest of hollow bosoms.

A plague of opinion.

A pond as deep as hell.

A promise-breaker.

A sign of dignity, a breath, a bubble.

A sin-absolver.

A snapper-up of unconsidered trifles.

A still-soliciting eye.

A thousand daggers in thy thoughts.

A very mean meaning.

Abstract of all faults.

Act of darkness.

Ah, how the poor world is pestered with such water-flies, diminutives of nature.

And to what metal this counterfeit lump of ore will be melted.

All goodness is poison to thy stomach.

An abuser of the world.

An angler in the lake of darkness.

Anointed sovereign of sighs and groans.
Arrogant piece of flesh.
Apes of idleness.
As dead midnight still.
As false, by heaven, as heaven itself is true.
As false coin.
As frozen water to a starved snake.
As naked as the vulgar air.
As the parasite's silk.
As well might poison poison.
Audacious cruelty.

B

Babbling gossip of the air.
Baited it with all the unmuzzled thoughts that
    tyrannous heart can think.
Banishment—the damned use that word in hell.
Base and ignominious treasons.
Bear themselves like foolish justices.
Bears a frosty sound.
Beautiful tyrant.
Begot of thought, conceived of spleen, and born of
    madness.
Black brow of night.
Black contagious breath.
Black defiance.
Black envy.
Black scandal, or foul-faced reproach.
Black word.
Blistered be thy tongue.

Blood-drinking hate.
Bloody looks.
Boiled to death with melancholy.
Breaker of proverbs.
Breathe foul contagious darkness in the air.
Bold and saucy wrong.
Brassy bosoms, and rough hearts of flint.
Brazen-faced varlet.
Burn in never-quenching fire.
Burning shame.
By underhand corrupted injustice.

C

Can vengeance be pursued further than death.
Canker'd hate.
Canker'd with peace.
Chop on some cold thought.
Civil butchery.
Clog of conscience and sour melancholy.
Close-tongued treason and the ravisher.
Closet-war.
Cloudy countenance.
Cold coward.
Cold-moving nods froze me into silence
Conceit deceitful.
Concupiscible intemperate lust.
Condemned into everlasting redemption.
Conscience wide as hell.
Conspire against destiny.
Contagious fogs.

Cracking the strong warrant of an oath.
Crept too near his conscience.

D

Damned blood-suckers.
Damned tripe-visaged rascal.
Damns himself to do, dares better be damned than
    to do it.
Dark as ignorance, though ignorance dark as hell.
Dark harbor for defame.
Deedless in his tongue.
Deep malice makes too deep incision.
Despised substance of divinest show.
Devilish policy.
Disdains the shadow.
Diffused infection of a man.
Disorder, horror, fear, and meeting.
Does buy and sell his honor as he pleases.
Dog-hearted.
Dost dialogue with thy shadow.
Doth almost persuade Justice to break her sword.
Dove feather'd raven.
Dragon wing of night.
Drinks the green mantle of the standing-pool.

E

Ear-kissing arguments.
Egregious indignity.

Endless liar, an hourly promise breaker, the owner of
no good quality.
Engines of lust.
Envenom him with words.
Envious barking of your saucy tongue.
Envious tongue.
Envious worm.
Eyeless night.

F

Faith infringed.
Faith, half asleep.
Fair payment for foul words is more than due.
False as water.
False gaze.
Falsehood to thy heart.
Falser than vows made in wine.
Fearful owl of death.
Fiend angelical.
Flint bosom.
For all the mud in Egypt.
Foul imaginary eyes of blood.
Foul-mouthed man.
Foul tainted flesh.
Foul throat.
Frozen conscience and hot-burning will.
Full of scorpions.
Full of new-found oaths, which he will break.

G

Glass-fac'd flatterer.
Glory grows guilty of detested crimes.
Grim cave of death.
Grinning honor.
Gross and miserable ignorance.
Guilty diligence.

H

Hag of all despite.
Hath sullied all his gloss of former honor.
Have secret feet.
He had a black mouth.
He hath a killing tongue.
He hath out-villained villainy.
He is a flatterer, a parasite, a keeper-back of death.
He takes false shadows for true substances.
He that depends upon your favor swims with fins of
    lead.
He was the very genius of famine.
He wears a key in his ear, and a lock hanging by it.
He watered his new plants with dews of flattery.
He will fence with his own shadow.
He will sell the fee-simple of his salvation.
Heinous, black, obscene a deed.
Hell-black night.
Hell gnaw his bones.
Helpless smoke of words.

His general behavior vain, ridiculous and thrasonical.
His discourse peremptory, his tongue filed.
Hollow eyes of death.

I

I am stiffed with this smell of sin.
I weigh it lightly, were it heavier.
Ignorant tongues.
If he be less, he's nothing; but he's more, had I more
　　name for badness.
In the sick air.
Ingrateful, savage, and inhuman creature.
Infect mine eyes.
Insupportable vexation.
Interior hatred.
Into a pit of ink.
Iron tongue and brazen mouth.
Iron-witted fools.
Irreligious piety.
Is crammed with arrogancy, spleen, and pride.
It is a manacle of love.
It is but his policy to counterfeit.
It is like a barber's chair, that fits all buttocks.
It is like a pardon after execution.
It proceeds from policy, not love.

J

Just opposite to what thou justly seem'st.

K

Knit poisonous clouds.

L

Lascivious apprehension.
Learned without opinion.
Less valiant than the virgin in the night.
Let all untruths stand by thy stained name, and
    they'll seem glorious.
Lie at my mercy.
Like captives bound to a triumphant car.
Like damned guilty deeds to sinner's minds.
Like the breath of unfeed lawyer.
Lily-liver'd boy.
Limber vows.
Lions make leopards tame, but not change his spots.
Lump of foul deformity.
Lust-dieted man.

M

Made impudent with use of evil deeds.
Make glory base, and sovereignity a slave.
Marble-hearted fiend.
Measureless liar.
Mechanical salt-butter rogue.
Men's evil manners live in brass, their virtues we
    write in water.
Milk-liver'd man.

Millions of false eyes.
Mingled with venom of suggestion.
Minister of hell.
Misery acquaints a man with strange bedfellows.
Monster ignorance.
Monstrous fault.
More fierce than empty tigers.
More haughty than the devil.
Mouth-made vows.
Murk and occidental damp.
My conscience hath a thousand several tongues.

N

Never changing night.
Night's black agents.
Night's black bosom.
No better than a sty.
No excuse current, but to hang thyself.
No sleep close up that deadly eye of thine.
No metal can bear half the keeness of thy sharp envy.
No more man's blood in his belly than will sup a flea.
No more mercy in him than there is milk in a male tiger.
Not yet so ugly a fiend of hell.
Nothing but songs of death.
Nursed by baseness.

O

Omnipotent villain.
Opposite to humanity.

Out from false fortune's frown.
Out of his self-drawing web.
Out, you green-sickness carrion.

P

Pain of perpetual displeasure.
Pale cold cowardice.
Paper-faced villain.
Paris is dirt to him.
Patched with foul moles and eye-offending marks.
Peace is to me a war.
Perfumed by a fen.
Pernicious ass.
Pernicious bloodsucker of sleeping men.
Pernicious rage.
Pernicious usurer, forward by nature, enemy to peace.
Perpetual shame.
Perpetual wink.
Pigeon-liver'd, and lack gall.
Played by the picture of Nobody.
Portrait of a blinking idiot.
Prove a deadly bloodshed but a jest.
Preposterous ass.
Preposterous and frantic outrage.
Purge you of your scum.

R

Ransacking the church, offending charity.
Rash gunpowder.

Red-tailed humble-bee.
Revenge—which makes the foul offender quake.
Riot and dishonor stain the brow.
Rotten smoke.
Ruin'd piece of nature.

S

Sacrificial whisperings.
Sad as night.
Sanctimonious ceremonies.
Sanguine coward, this bed-presser, this huge hell
    of flesh.
School of night.
Scurvy fellow.
Seek to unsphere the stars with oaths.
Serpent heart.
Shag-ear'd villain.
Shallow changing woman.
Shapeless idleness.
She is as forward of her breeding, as she is in the rear
    of your birth.
Should make desire vomit emptiness.
Slanderous tongue.
Slinking clothes that fretted in their own grease.
Slippery creatures.
Snift-taffeta fellow.
Spoke such scurvy and provoking terms.
Spoken untruths, secondarily.
So smooth he daubed his vice with a show of virtue.
Some cogging, cozening slave.

Son of utter darkness.
Sons of darkness.
Sought to entrap me by intelligence.
Soul's fair temple is defaced.
Striving to make an ugly deed look fair.
Stuffing the ears of men with false reports.
Sworn rioter.
Sullen black.
Superfluous leisure.

T

Take deep traitors for thy dearest friends.
Taint not thy mind.
Tainted with a thousand vices.
That bottled spider, that foul hunch-backed toad.
That broker that still breaks the pate of faith.
That daily break-vow.
That dog, that had his teeth before his eyes.
That errs in ignorance and not in cunning.
That foul defacer of God's handy-work.
That incestuous, that adulterate beast.
That purpose-changer, that sly devil.
The affair cries haste.
The cistern of my lust.
The clogging burden of a guilty soul.
The eye of heaven is out, and misty night.
The flattering index of a direful pageant.
The gnawing vulture of thy mind.
The ingredient is a devil.
The night is long that never finds the day.

The prince of darkness.
The root of his opinion, which is rotten.
The slave of nature, and the son of hell.
The tartness of his face sours ripe grapes.
The trumpet of our wrath.
The wide sea of my conscience.
The word is too good to paint out her wickedness.
The worm of conscience still be-gnaw thy soul.
There can be no kernel in this light nut.
There is no leprosy but what thou speakest.
There souls are topfull of offence.
There's a double tongue.
They have verified unjust things.
They shoot but calm words, folded up in smoke.
This offer comes from mercy, not from fear.
This milky gentleness.
This ravenous tiger, this accursed devil.
Thou art poison to my blood.
Thou blow'st the fire when temperance is thaw'd.
Thou core of envy.
Thou did'st bear the key of all my counsels.
Thou disease of a friend.
Thou foul abetter, thou notorious bawd.
Thou furnace of foul-reeking smoke.
Thou globe of sinful continents.
Thou green sarcenet flap for a sore eye.
Thou idle immaterial skein of sley'd silk.
Thou issue of a mangy dog.
Thou liest in reputation sick.
Thou mak'st the vestal violate her oath.
Thou plantest scandal, and displacest laud.

Thou rag of honor.
Thou ravisher, thou traitor, thou false thief.
Thou smother'st honesty, thou murder'st troth.
Thou tassel of a prodigal's purse.
Threatening eye.
Through the false passage of thy throat, thou liest.
Thy bed, lust-stain'd, shall with lust's blood be
     spotted.
Thy deed, inhuman and unnatural.
Thy honey turns to gall, thy joy to grief.
Thy private feasting to a public fast.
Thy secret pleasure turns to open shame.
Thy sin's not accidental, but a trade.
Thy smoothing titles to a ragged name.
Thy sugar'd tongue to bitter wormwood taste.
Thy violent vanities can never last.
Tiger-footed rage.
Toad-spotted traitor.
To dwell in solemn shades of endless night.
Tongue spit their duties out, and cold hearts freeze.
Tongue-tied sorrows.
Tragic volume.
Treason and murder ever kept together.
True-bred cowards as ever turned back.
Turn her virtue into pitch.
Turned an eye of death.

U

Unmannerly sadness.
Unruly spleen.

Unsubstantial air.
Unthread the rude eye of rebellion.
Untimely violence.
Untun'd tongue.

V

Valiant ignorance.
Varnish'd faces.
Vast sin-concealing chaos.
Vicious qualities.
Vile reproach.
Vilely compil'd.
Villainous abominable misleader of youth.
Villains that do stand by thee are pure.
Viperous slander.
Virgin-violator.
Virtuous lie.
Vulgar wisdom.
Vulgar wit.
Vulture of sedition.

W

Walks like contempt.
Was ever book containing such vile matter.
What a spendthrift is he of his tongue.
Where death and danger dog the heels of worth.
Where shame doth harbor.
Which swims against your stream of quality.
Whispering conspirator.

Whose gall coins slanders like a mint.
Whose hard heart is button'd up with steel.
Whose nature sickens but to speak of truth.
Whose sole name blisters our tongue.
Wicked heinous fault.
Wipe off the lust that hides our scepter's gilt.
With foreheads villainous low.
With swifter spleen than powder can enforce.
With the spleen of all the under fiends.
Wolvish-ravening lamb.
Worse than any name.
Wonderful, when devils tell the truth.
Would thou wert clean enough to spit upon.
Wound that nothing healeth.

Y

You always end ere you begin.
You bawling, blasphemous, uncharitable dog.
You cannot make gross sins look clear.
You filthy famished correctioner.
You have as little honesty as honor.
You rat-catcher.
You shall digest the venom of your spleen.
You tallow face.
You whoreson indistinguishable cur.
Your company is fairer than honest.
Your reasons have been sharp and sententious.

SECTION IV

∽

EPIGRAMS

A

A beggar's book out-worths a noble's blood.
A dream itself is but a shadow.
A fool's bolt is soon shot.
A friend should bear his friend's infirmities.
A golden mind stoops not to shows of dross.
A good wit will make use of anything.
A heavy heart bears not a nimble tongue.
A lover's eyes will gaze an eagle blind.
A subtle traitor needs no sophister.
A truth's a truth.
A woman mov'd is like a fountain troubled.
A woman's thought runs before her action.
After life's fitful fever he sleeps well.
All that glisters is not gold.
All's not offense that indiscretion finds.
An honest tale speeds best, being plainly told.
And thrift is blessing, if men steal it not.
And where care lodges, sleep will never lie.

B

Best safety lies in fear.
Better a little chiding than a great deal of
  heart-breaking.
Better a witty fool than a foolish wit.
Better once than never, for never too late.

Better three hours too soon than a minute too late.
Brevity is the soul of wit.
But every rub is smoothed on our way.

C

Can one desire too much of a good thing?
Can virtue hide itself?
Comfort comes too late; it is like a pardon after
    execution.
Could beauty, my lord, have better commerce than
    with honesty?
Courage mounteth with occasion.
Curses never pass the lips of those that breathe them
    in the air.

D

Death of one person can be paid but once.
Deep sounds make lesser noise than shallow-fords.
Die single, and thine image dies with thee.
Divorce not wisdom from your honor.
Do not lend money upon bare friendship, without
    security.
Dull not device by coldness and delay.

E

Every man has his fault.
Everyman's conscience is a thousand men.

F

Familiarity will grow more contempt.

Few love to hear the sin they love to act.

Fire that's closest kept burns most of all.

For sorrow ends not when it seemeth done.

For truth hath better deeds than words to grace it.

Forbear to judge, for we are sinners all.

Fortune brings in some boats that are not steer'd.

Fortune reigns in gifts of the world, not in the
lineaments of nature.

Foul deeds will rise, though all the earth o'erwhelm
them, to men's eyes.

Friendly counsel cuts off many foes.

From iron came music's origin.

Full oft we see cold wisdom waiting on superfluous
folly.

G

Good effects may spring from words of love.

Great men oft die by vile contempt.

H

Happy are they that hear their detractions and can
put them to mending.

He lives in fame that died in virtue's cause.

He needs no cunning that for truth doth fight.

He that is giddy thinks the world turns round.

He that loves to be flattered is worthy o' the flatterer.

He who dies pays all debts.
Honest, plain words best pierce the ear of grief.
Hope is a lover's staff; walk hence with that.
How long a time lies in one little word.
How use doth breed a habit in a man.

I

I am not fair; and therefore I pray the gods make me
    honest.
I am wealthy in my friends.
I hourly learn a doctrine of obedience.
I learn to read what silent love hath writ.
I will praise any man that will praise me.
I would my horse had the speed of your tongue.
If you love her, you cannot see her. Love Is blind.
Ill blows the wind that profits nobody.
In a false quarrel there is no true valor.
In himself he is.
In nature's infinite book of secrecy a little I can read.
In time we hate that which we often fear.
It is a wise father that knows his own child.

J

Jesters do oft prove prophets.

K

Keep yourself within yourself.
Knowledge the wing wherewith we fly to heaven.

L

Law itself is perfect wrong.
Let her beauty be her wedding-dower.
Let your mind be coupled with your words.
Love looks not with the eyes, but with the mind.
Love-thoughts lie rich, when canopied with bowers.
Love's fire heats water, water cools not love.
Love's reason's without reason.

M

Man and wife, being two, are one in love.
Man breaks his neck in vain glory.
Man takes false shadows for true substances.
Many a good hanging prevents a bad marriage.
Men are merriest when they are from home.
Men at some time are masters of their fates.
Men have no wings to fly from God.
Men lose when they incline to treachery.
Men of few words are the best men.
Minds sway'd by eyes are full of turpitude.
Misery acquaints a man with strange bedfellows.
My cause and honor guard me.
My idleness doth hatch.

N

No beast so fierce but knows some touch of pity.
No evil lost is wail'd when it is gone.
No man is the lord of anything.

Nothing can be made out of nothing.
Nothing can seem foul to those that win.
Nothing emboldens sin so much as mercy.
Nothing will come of nothing.

O

O, how full of briars is this working-day world.
O, I do not like that paying back; 't is a double labor.
Of all base passions, fear is most accurs'd.
Oh, who can find the bent of woman's fancy.
One doth not know how much an ill word may
    empoison.

P

Plenty, and peace, breeds cowards.
Poor women's faces are their own faults' books.
Present fears are less than horrible imaginings.
Pride must have a fall.

R

Rich gifts wax poor when givers prove unkind.

S

Screw your courage to the sticking place.
Self-charity be sometimes a vice.
She died, my lord, but whiles her slander liv'd.
Silence is the perfectest herald of joy.
Silver hairs will purchase us a good opinion.

Slander lives upon succession.

Small things make base men proud.

Society is no comfort to one not sociable.

So sweet is zealous contemplation.

Some men have a killing tongue, but a quiet sword.

Some people are as innocent as grace itself.

Some people have angel's faces, but heaven knows
 their hearts.

Sometimes I and my bosom must debate a while.

Striving to better, oft we mar what's well.

Strong reasons make strange actions.

Sweet mercy is nobility's true badge.

Suspicion, all our lives, shall be stuck full of eyes.

T

Talkers are no good doers; be assured.

Tears do not become a man.

Tears show their love, but want their remedies.

The better part of valor is discretion.

The course of true love never did run smooth.

The cuckoo builds not for himself.

The dullness of the fool is the whetstone of the wits.

The empty vessel makes the greatest sound.

The path is smooth that leadeth on to danger.

The sands are numbered that make up life.

The sea hath bounds, but deep desire hath none.

The service and the loyalty, I owe, in doing it,
 pays itself.

The will of man is by his reason sway'd.

The world is full of rubs.

The world, they lose it that do buy it with much care.

There are many sharp reasons to defeat the law.

There is no darkness but ignorance.

There is no virtue like necessity.

There's beggary in the love that can be reckon'd.

There's daggers in men's smiles.

There's difference in no persons.

There's none can truly say he gives, if he receives.

There's small choice in rotten apples.

They laugh that win.

They love not poison that do poison need.

They love thee not that use thee.

They stumble that run fast.

They that thrive will take counsel of their friends.

Things sweet to taste prove in digestion sour.

Things won are done; joy's soul lies in the doing.

Time goes on crutches till love have all his rites.

Time shall unfold what plighted cunning hides.

To be once in doubt is once to be resolv'd.

Tongues of men are full of deceits.

True nobility is exempt from fear.

Truth hath a quiet breast.

Two may keep counsel when the third's away.

Two women placed together makes cold weather.

U

Unbidden guests are often welcomest when they are
    gone.

Unkindness strikes a deeper wound than steel.

W

We are in God's hands.

We are time's subjects, and time bids begone.

We speak not what we mean.

We were born to die.

What I am, and what I would, are secrets.

What should I do, I do not.

What touches us ourself shall be last serv'd.

What's aught but as 't is valued.

What's in the brain that ink may character.

When no friends are by, men praise themselves.

Who is 't can read a woman.

Who hates honor, hates the gods above.

Wisdom cries out in the street, and no man regards
it.

Wives may be merry and yet honest too.

Who ever lov'd that lov'd hot at first sight.

Woman is no stronger than her sex.

Words pay no debts.

Y

Yet youth, the more it is wasted the sooner it wears.

You can do better yet.

You cannot shun yourself.

You cannot tell who's your friend.

You have the grace of God, sir, and he hath enough.

Your mind is all as youthful as your blood.

Your own glass shows you, when you look in it.

SECTION V

INTERESTING EXPRESSIONS WHICH HAVE NO SPECIAL CLASSIFICATION

I will bite my thumb at them;
Which is a disgrace to them
If they bear it.

You kiss by the book.

I will dry-beat you with an iron wit,
And put up my iron dagger.

—ROMEO AND JULIET

⤫

A dream itself is but a shadow.
Truly, and I hold ambition of so airy
And light a quality, that it is but a
Shadow's shadow.

We do sugar o'er the devil himself.

This is the very coinage of your brain.

I must be cruel, only to be kind.

If words be made of breath
And breath of life, I have no life to breathe
What thou hast said to me.

Whom I will trust, as I will adders fang'd.

A knavish speech sleeps in a foolish ear.

The body is with the king, but the king
is not with the body. The king is a thing.

Diseases, desperate grown.
By desperate appliance are reliev'd.

Hamlet has just killed Polonius. We listen to the
following conversation between the king and Hamlet:

King.　　Now, Hamlet, where's Polonius?
Hamlet.　At supper.
King.　　At supper? Where?

Hamlet.　Not where he eats, but where he is eaten:
a certain convocation of politic worms are e'en at him. Your
worm is your only emperor for diet; we fat all creatures else,
to fat us; and we fat ourselves for maggots: Your fat king,
and your lean beggar, is but variable service; two dishes,
but to one table; that's the end.

A man may fish with the worm that hath eat of a
king; and eat of the fish that hath fed of that worm!

Conjures the wandering stars.
And makes them stand.

Until my eyelids will no longer wag.

—Hamlet, Prince of Denmark

༄

I would advise you to shift a shirt.

I would have broke mine eye-strings; crack'd them,

But to look upon him; till the diminution
Of space had pointed him sharp as my needle;
Nay, follow'd him, till he had melted from
The smallness of a gnat to air.

What shall thou expect.
To be depender on a thing that leans.

Fold down the leaf where I have left.

It is a voice in her ears, which horse-hairs and
calves'-guts, nor the voice of unpaved eunuch to boot,
can never amend.

Must wear the print of his remembrance out.

Not Hercules
Could have knock'd out his brains, for he had none.

Meet the time, as it seeks us.

Unless a man would marry a gallows, and beget
young gibbets.

By medicine life may be prolong'd, yet death
Will seize the doctor too.

—Cymbeline

The affair cries haste.

Cables of perdurable toughness.

She puts her tongue a little in her heart, and chides
with thinking.

You rise to play, and go to bed to work.

I am not merry; but I do beguile
The thing I am, by seeming otherwise.

O heavy ignorance!—thou praisest the worst best.

Knavery's plain face is never seen till us'd.

Reputation is an idle and most false imposition;
Oft got without merit, and lost without deserving.

Had I as many mouths as Hydra such an answer
would stop them all.

He shall in strangeness stand no farther than in a
politic distance.

To have him see me woman'd.

They laugh that win.

O, she will sing the savageness out of a bear.

If that the earth could teem with woman's tears,
Each drop she falls would prove a crocodile.

Well-painted passion.

Whom passion could not shake? whose solid virtue
The shot of accident, nor dart of chance.
Could neither graze, nor pierce?

He is that he is: I may not breathe my censure.
What he might be,—if, what he might, he is not,—
I would to heaven, he were.

If she be not honest, and true,
There's no man happy; the purest of their wives
Is foul as slander.

Steep'd me in poverty to the very lips.

Not to pick bad from bad; but, by bad, mend!

Smooth as monumental alabaster.

She was false as water.

As ignorant as dirt.

For thou hast kill'd the sweetest innocent
That e'er did lift up eye.

Of one that lov'd not wisely, but too well.

—OTHELLO

❧

When we for recompense have prais'd the vile.
It stains the glory in that happy verse
Which aptly sings the good.

I am not of that feather, to shake off
My friend when he must need me.

His honesty rewards him in itself.

Our own precedent passions do instruct us
What levity's in youth.

You mend the jewel by the wearing it.

You had rather be at a breakfast of enemies, than a
dinner of friends.

There is no crossing him in his humor.

'Tis pity bounty had not eyes behind;
That man might ne'er be wretched for his mind.

Four milk-white horses, trapp'd in silver.

That what he speaks is all in debt, he owes for every
    word;
He is so kind, that he now pays interest for it.

                    Friendship's full of dregs:
Methinks, false hearts should never have sound legs.
Thus honest fools lay out their wealth on courtesies.

She's e'en setting on water to scald such chickens as
    you are.

As much foolery as I have, so much wit thou lackest.

An honor in him, which buys out his fault.

Pity is the virtue of the law.
And none but tyrants use it cruelly.

The unkindest beast more kinder than mankind.

                    I do wish thou wert a dog,
That I might love thee something.

   Promise me friendship, but perform none: If thou
wilt not promise, the gods plague thee, for thou art a
man! if thou dost perform, confound thee, for thou'rt
a man!

Were I like thee I'd throw away myself.

Thou hast cast away thyself, being like thyself.

And the spots on thy kindred were jurors on thy life.

Whose blush doth thaw the consecrated snow
That lies on Dian's lap!

Methinks, thou art more honest now than wise.

Performance is a kind of will, or testament,
Which argues a great sickness in his judgment
That makes it.

Wilt thou whip thine own faults in other men?

What a gods' gold
that he is worshipp'd in a baser temple,
Than where swine feed!

Graves only be men's works; and death their gain!

—Timon of Athens

He that keeps nor crust nor crumb.
Weary of all, shall want some.

O good man's fortune may grow out heels.

Lend me a looking-glass;
If that her breath will moist or stain the stone,
Why, then she lives.

—King Lear

> 'T is the eye of childhood
That fears a painted devil.

Modest wisdom plucks me from over-credulous haste.

The night is long that never finds the day.

He cannot buckle his distemper'd cause
Within the belt of rule.

—MACBETH

It is too starv'd a subject for my sword.

If you love an addle egg as well as you love an idle head, you would eat chicken i' the shell.

Paris is dirt to him.

The wound of peace is surity.

You fur your gloves with reason.

The elephant hath joints, but none for courtesy.

His silence drinks up his applause.

The fool slides o'er the ice that you should break.

He raves in saying nothing.

My mind is troubled, like a fountain stirr'd;
And I myself see not the bottom of it.

Would I were as deep under the earth as I am
above!

I'll take that winter from your lips fair lady.

It is the purpose that makes strong the vow.

—TROILUS AND CRESSIDA

What custom wills, in all things should we do 't,
The dust on antique time would lie unswept.
And mountainous error be too highly heap'd
For truth to overpeer.

I would have had you put your power well on.
Before you had worn it out.

The virtue of your name is not here passable.

Though it were as virtuous to he as to live chastely.

As if a man were author of himself.

O, a kiss long as my exile, sweet as my revenge!

I hope to frame thee.

As certain as I know the sun is fire.

—CORIOLANUS

A surgeon to old shoes.

Cæsar talking to Brutus:
It is very much lamented, Brutus,
That you have no such mirrors as will turn

Your hidden worthiness into your eye.
That you might see your shadow.

My life is run his compass.

—JULIUS CÆSAR

⌒⌒

You can do better yet.

That I might sleep out this great gap of time.

Be a child o' the time.

Our fortune lies upon this jump.

And I, an ass, am onion-eyed; for shame.

   The devil himself will not eat a woman: . . . A woman
is a dish for the gods, if the devil dress her not . . . In
every ten that they make, the devils mar five.

—ANTONY AND CLEOPATRA

⌒⌒

Thine eye darts forth the fire that burneth me.

As apt as new-fallen snow takes any dint.

The wolf doth grin before it barketh.

In night, desire sees best of all.

—VENUS AND ADONIS

As is the morning's silver-melting dew
Against the golden splendor of the sun!
An expir'd date, cancell'd ere well begun.

For by our ears our hearts oft tainted be.

For unstain'd thoughts do seldom dream
Birds never limed no secret bushes fear.

Then my digression is so vile, so base
That it will live engraven in my face.

Her hair, like golden threads, play'd with her breath

Her azure veins, her alabaster skin,
Her coral lips, her snow-white dimpled chin.

Her breasts, like ivory globes with blue,
A pair of maiden worlds unconquered,
Save of their lord no bearing yoke they knew,
And him by oath they truly honored.
These worlds in Tarquin new ambition bred.

Light and lust are deadly enemies.

Pure Chastity is rifled of her store,
And Lust, the thief, far poorer than before.

And waste huge stones with little water-drops.

The crow may bathe his coal-black wings in mire,
And unperceiv'd fly with the filth away,
But if the like the snow-white swan desire,
The stain upon his silver down will stay.

> Poor grooms are sightless night, kings glorious day.
> Gnats are unnoted wheresoe'er they fly,
> But eagles gaz'd upon with every eye.
>
> Deep sounds make lesser noise than shallow fords,
> And sorrow ebbs, being blown with wind of words.

About him were a press of gaping faces
Which seem'd to swallow up his sound advice.

The poison'd fountain clears itself again.

—THE RAPE OF LUCRECE

✺

Die single, and thine image dies with thee.

O learn to read what silent love hath writ.

Which, like a jewel hung in ghastly night,
Makes black night beauteous, and her old face new.

> Full many a glorious morning have I seen
> Flatter the mountain-tops with sovereign eye.
> Kissing with golden face the meadows green,
> Gilding pale streams with heavenly alchemy;
> Anon permit the basest clouds to ride
> With ugly rack on his celestial face,
> And from the forlorn world his visage hide,
> Stealing unseen to west with this disgrace.
>
> No more be griev'd at that which thou hast done:
> Roses have thorns, and silver fountains mud;
> Clouds and eclipses stain both moon and sun,
> And loathsome canker lives in sweetest bud.

All days are nights to see, till I see thee,
   And nights, bright days, when dreams do show thee me.

On Helen's cheek all art of beauty set.

Like as the waves make towards the pebbled shore
So do our minutes hasten to their end.

So all my best is dressing old words new,
Spending again what is already spent.

There lives more life in one of your fair eyes
Than both your poets can in praise devise.

Give not a windy night a rainy morrow.

   Some glory in their birth, some in their skill,
   Some in their wealth, some in their body's force;
   Some in their garments, though new-fangled ill;
   Some in their hawks and hounds, some in their horse;
   And every human hath his adjunct pleasure.
   Wherein it finds a joy above the rest;
   But these particulars are not my measure,
   All these I better in one general best.
   Thy love is better than high birth to me,

   Richer than wealth, prouder than garments cost,
   Of more delight than hawks and horses be;
   And having thee, of all men's pride I boast.

Where beauty's veil doth cover every blot.

The hardest knife ill-used doth lose his edge.

Love is too young to know what conscience is;
Yet who knows not, conscience is born of love.

                    —SONNETS

What a hell of witchcraft lies
In the small orb of one particular tear!

—A Lover's Complaint

❧

Fair is my love, but not so fair as fickle;
Mild as a dove, but neither true nor trusty;
Brighter than glass, and yet, as glass is, brittle;
Softer than wax, and yet, as iron, rusty:
    A lily pale, with damask die to grace her,
    None fairer, nor none falser to deface her.

Her lips to mine how often hath she join'd,
Between each kiss her oaths of true love swearing!
How many tales to please me hath she coin'd,
Dreading any love, the loss thereof still fearing!
    Yet in the midst of all her pure protestings,
    Her faith, her oaths, her tears, and all were jestings.

—The Passionate Pilgrim

❧

Love's a mighty lord.

      She is mine own:
And I as rich in having such a jewel,
As twenty seas, if all their sand were pearl,
The water nectar, and the rocks pure gold.

For love, thou know'st, is full of jealousy.

Didst thou but know'st the inly touch of love,
Thou would'st as soon go kindle fire with snow,
As such to quench the fire of love with words.

Wilt thou reach stars, because they shine on thee?

To be slow in words is a woman's only virtue.

—THE TWO GENTLEMEN OF VERONA

As swift as lead.

A lover's eyes will gaze an eagle blind.

And, when love speaks, the voice of all the gods
Makes heaven drowsy with the harmony.

The letter is too long by half a mile.

We number nothing that we spend for you;
Our duty is so rich, so infinite,
That we may do it still without accompt.
Vouchsafe to show the sunshine of your face,
That we, like savages, may worship it.

The tongues of mocking wenches are as keen
As is the razor's edge invisible.

Ay, if he have no more man's blood in 's belly than
    will sup a flea.

—LOVE'S LABOR'S LOST

The appetite of her eye did seem to scorch me up like
   a burning glass!

I will be, as sure as his guts are made of pudding.

It makes me almost ready to wrangle with mine own
   honesty.

Pluck the borrowed veil of modesty.

I'll have my brains ta'en out, and butter'd, and give
   them to a dog for a new year's gift.

They say there is divinity in odd numbers.

Better a little chiding than a great deal of heartbreak.

As poor as Job.

              — THE MERRY WIVES OF WINDSOR

⤳

I to the world am like a drop of water,
That in the ocean seeks another drop;
Who, falling there to find his fellow forth,
Unseen, inquisitive, confounds himself.

Have at you with a proverb.

It is a fault that springeth from your eye.

Some devils ask but the paring of one's nail.

And careful hours, with Time's deformed hand,
Have written strange defeatures in my face.

              — THE COMEDY OF ERRORS

Rids his hands of her.

Believe me, sir, they butt together well.

— THE TAMING OF THE SHREW

Quench'd in the chaste beams of the watery moon.

Thy love ne'er alter, till thy sweet life end.

A lion among ladies.

Pluck the wings from painted butterflies.

The iron tongue of midnight hath told twelve.

—A MIDSUMMER NIGHT'S DREAM

When he is best he is a little worse than a man;
And when he is worst he is little better than a beast.

You have the grace of God, and he hath enough.

Lovers ever run before the clock.

O that I had a title good enough to keep his name
   company.

I would not have given it for a wilderness of monkeys.

All the wealth I had ran in my veins.

This making of Christians will raise the price of hogs.

—THE MERCHANT OF VENICE

Where unclean mind carries virtuous qualities,
There commendations go with pity.

The gift doth stretch itself as 't is receiv'd.

I grow to you, and our parting is a tortured body.

I shall now put you to the height of your breeding.

There can be no kernel in this light nut;
The soul of this man is his clothes.

I am no great Nebuchadnezzar, sir, I have not much
skill in grass.

She knew her distance, and did angle for me.

This woman's an easy glove, she goes off and on at
pleasure.

—ALL'S WELL THAT ENDS WELL

*

I would my horse had the speed of your tongue!

I could not endure a husband with a beard on his face.

Thy wit is as quick as the grayhound's mouth, it
catches.

—MUCH ADO ABOUT NOTHING

*

Babbling gossip of the air.

What is decreed must be.

Go shake your ears.

I have wit enough to lie straight in my bed.

> For women are as roses; whose fair flower,
> Being once display'd, doth fall that very hour.

Let me be boiled to death with melancholy.

He has been yonder i' the sun, practising behavior to his own shadow.

I thank my stars I am happy.

> My desire,
> More sharp than filed steel, did spur me forth.

It is something of my negligence, nothing of my purpose.

Some are born great, some achieve greatness, and some have greatness thrown upon them.

—Twelfth Night; or, What You Will

✦

Fortune reigns in gifts of the world, not in the lineaments of nature.

Now unmuzzle your wisdom.

> I shall ne'er be 'ware of mine own wit,
> Till I break my shins against it.

You'll be rotten ere you be half ripe.

Mar no more trees with writing love-songs in their barks.

What stature is she of?
Just as high as my heart.

That was begot of thought, conceived of spleen,
And born of madness.

Rich honesty dwells like a miser, sir, in a poor-house;
As your pearl, in your foul oyster.

—As You Like It

Thou concludest like the sanctimonious pirate, that
    went to sea with the ten commandments but
    scraped one out of the table.

Have worn your eyes almost out in the service.

Though 't is my familiar sin.

Our doubts are traitors,
And make us lose the good we oft might win,
    by fearing to attempt.

        To draw with idle spider's strings
        Most pond'rous and substantial things.

It is no other!

Against the tooth of time.

Be not so hot.

—Measure for Measure

Will you take eggs for money?

The bug which you would fright me with I seek.

Let my name be put in the book of virtue.

— THE WINTER'S TALE

⌒∽◯

I have great comfort from this fellow:
Methinks he hath no drowning mark upon him.

Your tale, sir, would cure deafness.

From mine own library, with volumes that I prize
   above my dukedom.

Mum then, and no more.

What a pied ninny 's this!

— THE TEMPEST

⌒∽◯

They shoot but calm words folded up in smoke.

As naked as the vulgar air.

Law itself is perfect wrong.

Doth move the murmuring lips of discontent.

Think you I bear the shears of destiny?
Have I commandment on the pulse of life?

The copy of your speed is learn'd by them.

—KING JOHN

For sorrow ends not when it seemeth done.

Should dying men flatter with those that live?
No, no; men living flatter those that die.

Thou liest in reputation sick.

His tongue is now a stringless instrument.

In war, was never lion rag'd more fierce,
In peace, was never gentle lamb more mild.

Of much less value is my company than your good
    words . . . .
Your presence makes us rich.

And darts his light through every guilty hole.

Blushing discontented sun.

Better far off, than near, be ne'er the near.

Piece the way out with a heavy heart.

His prayers are full of false hypocrisy;
Ours of true zeal and deep integrity.

—KING RICHARD II

I am a bunch of radish.

I see virtue in his looks.

I'll cavil on the ninth part of a hair.

Never-dying honor.

I am heinously unprovided.

Thou art the king of honor.

With tears of innocency, and terms of zeal.

Suspicion, all our lives, shall be stuck full of eyes.

Grinning honor.

We will not trust our eyes without our ears.

> If a lie may do thee grace,
> I'll gild it with the happiest terms I have.

—KING HENRY IV, PART I

⁓

He seem'd in running to devour the way.

I were better to be eaten to death with rust, than to
be scoured to nothing with perpetual motion.

I kiss thee with a most constant heart.

Perfumed chambers of the great.

The son of the female is the shadow of the male.

Thou wilt be as valiant as the wrathful dove, or most
magnanimous mouse.

Their eyes of fire sparkling through sights of steel.

Our peace will, like broken limb united.
Grow stronger for the breaking.

I have a whole school of tongues in this belly of mine.

I have speeded hither with the very extremest inch
   of possibility.

I have him already tempering between my finger and
   my thumb.

Turning past evils to advantages.

Which swims against your stream of quality.

Fill the cup, and let it come;
I'll pledge you a mile to the bottom.

Doff'd the world aside, and let it pass.

—KING HENRY IV, PART II

∽

That what you speak is in your conscience washed
As pure as sin with baptism.

All out of work, and cold for action.

Ripe for exploits and mighty enterprises.

Yet that is but a crushed necessity.

Men are merriest when they are from home.

Every rub is smoothed on our way.

Pick'd from the worm-holes of long-vanish'd days,
Nor from the dust of old oblivion rak'd.

He'll drop his heart into the sink of fear.

Swear by her foot, that she may tread out the oath.

I and my bosom must debate a while.

You may as well go about to turn the sun to ice, with
    fanning in his face with a peacock's feather.

And all my mother came into mine eyes.

Swift as stones enforced from the old Assyrian slings.

—KING HENRY V

King Henry the fifth, too famous to live long.

We will not fly, but to our enemies' throats.

The sun with one eye vieweth all the world.

Using no other weapon but his name.

The truth appears so naked on my side,
That any purblind eye may find it out . . .
And on my side it is so well apparell'd,
So clear, so shining, and so evident,
That it will glimmer through a blind man's eye.

Burns under feigned ashes of forg'd love.

Hath sullied all his gloss of former honor.

O, were mine eye-balls into bullets turn'd,
That I, in rage, might shoot them at your face!

—KING HENRY VI, PART I

Could I come near your beauty with my nails,
I'd set my ten commandments in your face.

The purest spring is not so free from mud.

My brain, more busy than the laboring spider.

He need not fear the sword, for his coat is of proof.

Hath gelded the commonwealth, and made it an
eunuch.

Let's kill all the lawyers.

—KING HENRY VI, PART II

'T is but his policy to counterfeit.

That's a day longer than a wonder lasts.

Where, having nothing, nothing he can lose.

We'll yoke together, like a double shadow.

I will charm your tongue.

— KING HENRY VI, PART III

Amorous looking glass.

I was too hot to do somebody good.

Right, as snow in harvest.

Idle weeds are fast in growth.

I weigh it lightly, were it heavier.

For by his face straight shall you know his heart.

Murder thy breath in middle of a word.

I enjoy the golden dew of sleep.

Tut, tut, thou art all ice, thy kindness freezes.

Well skill'd in curses.

Shallow changing woman.

We must have knocks.

—KING RICHARD III

Ere you ask, is given.

Many sharp reasons to defeat the law.

Heaven has an end in all.

With your theme, I could o'ermount the lark.

Believe it.

Hoods make not monks.

Believe it, this is true.

The honey of his language.

The prime man of the state.

O negligence fit for a fool to fall by!

All goodness is poison to thy stomach.

Some little memory of me will stir him.

Men's evil manners live in brass; their virtues
We write in water.

'T is like a pardon after execution.

                    He has strangled
His language in his tears.

                              —KING HENRY VIII

⚬

Sweet cell of virtue and nobility,
How many sons of mine hast thou in store.

And fame's eternal date, for virtue's praise.

These words are razors to my wounded heart.

Thy wit wants edge.

As unrelenting flint to drops of rain.

Like a taper in some monument.

There is enough written upon this earth
To stir a meeting in the mildest thoughts.

What a thing it is to be an ass.

Two may keep counsel when the third's away.

To ease the gnawing vulture of thy mind.

                              —TITUS ANDRONICUS

Or till the Destinies do cut his throat of life.

Like a poor man's right in the law.

Believe, I will.

That wants breathing too.

The pregnant instrument of wrath.

For truth can never be confirm'd enough,
Though doubts did ever sleep.

—PERICLES

⤬

I stamp this kiss upon the current lip.

Be masters of our manners.

This world's a city, full of straying streets
And death's the market-place, where each one meets.

Making misery their mirth, and affliction a toy to
     jest at.

A rose is the very emblem of a maid:
For when the west wind courts her gently,
How modestly she blows, and paints the sun
With her chaste blushes! When the north comes near
     her,
Rude and impatient, then, like chastity,
She locks her beauties in her bud again,
And leaves him to base briers.

My wife is jealous as a turkey.

Swifter than wind upon a field of corn.

And when you bark, do it with judgment.

As mad as a March hare.

My cause and honor guard me.

Ev'n with an eye-glance to choke Mar's drum.

See a wren hawk at a fly.

—THE TWO NOBLE KINSMEN

The surest way to charm a woman's tongue,
Is—break her neck.

—A YORKSHIRE TRAGEDY

SECTION VI

PHILOSOPHY

The earth, that's nature's mother, is her tomb;
What is her burying grave, that is her womb:
And from her womb children of divers kind
We sucking on her natural bosom find:
Many for many virtues excellent,
None but for some, and yet all different.
O, mickle is the powerful grace, that lies
In herbs, plants, stones, and their true qualities:
For nought so vile that on the earth doth live,
But to the earth some special good doth give;
Nor aught so good, but, strain'd from that fair use,
Revolts from true birth, stumbling on abuse:
Virtue itself turns vice, being misapplied;
And vice sometime's by action dignified.
Within the infant rind of this weak flower
Poison hath residence, and med'cine power:
For this, being smelt, with that part cheers each part;
Being tasted, slays all senses with the heart.
Two such opposed kings encamp them still
In man as well as herbs,—grace, and rude will;
And, where the worser is predominant,
Full soon the canker death eats up that plant.

—ROMEO AND JULIET

All things that we ordained festival,
Turn from their office to black funeral:

Our instruments to melancholy bells:
Our wedding cheer to a sad burial feast;
Our solemn hymns to sullen dirges change:
Our bridal flower serve for a buried corse,
And all things change them to the contrary.

—ROMEO AND JULIET

POLONIUS TO LAERTES

Give thy thoughts no tongue,
Nor any unproportion'd thought his act.
Be thou familiar, but by no means vulgar;
The friends thou hast, and their adoption tried,
Grapple them to thy soul with hoops of steel;
But do not dull thy palm with entertainment
Of each new-hatch'd, unfledg'd comrade. Beware
Of entrance to a quarrel, but, being in,
Bear 't that the opposed may beware of thee.

Give every man thine ear, but few thy voice;
Take each man's censure, but reserve thy judgment.
Costly thy habit as thy purse can buy,
But not express'd in fancy; rich, not gaudy;
For the apparel oft proclaims the man.

Neither a borrower, nor a lender be:
For loan oft loses both itself and friend,
And borrowing dulls the edge of husbandry.
This above all: to thine own self be true,

And it must follow, as the night the day,
Thou canst not then be false to any man.

—HAMLET, PRINCE OF DENMARK

⚬⌒⚬

PRACTICE WHAT YOU PREACH

Do not, as some ungracious pastors do,
Show me the steep and thorny way to heaven;
Whilst like a puff'd and reckless libertine,
Himself the primrose path of dalliance treads,
And recks not his own read.

—HAMLET, PRINCE OF DENMARK

⚬⌒⚬

HAMLET'S SOLILOQUY

To be, or not to be: that is the question:
Whether 't is nobler in the mind to suffer
The slings and arrows of outrageous fortune,
Or to take arms against a sea of troubles,
And by opposing end them? To die: to sleep;
No more; and, by a sleep, to say we end
The heartache and the thousand natural shocks
That flesh is heir to—'t is a consummation
Devoutly to be wished.

　　　　　To die, to sleep;
To sleep: perchance to dream: ay, there's the rub;

For in that sleep of death what dreams may come,
When we have shuffled off this mortal coil,
Must give us pause: there's the respect
That makes calamity of so long life;
For who would bear the whips and scorns of time,
The oppressor's wrong, the proud man's contumely,
The pangs of despis'd love, the law's delay,
The insolence of office, and the spurns
That patient merit of the unworthy takes,
When he himself might his quietus make
With a bare bodkin?

    Who would fardels bear,
To grunt and sweat under a weary life,
But that the dread of something after death,
The undiscover'd country from whose bourn
No traveler returns, puzzles the will,
And makes us rather bear those ills we have
Than fly to others that we know not of?

Thus conscience does make cowards of us all;
And thus the native hue of resolution
Is sicklied o'er with the pale cast of thought,
And enterprises of great pith and moment
With this regard their currents turn awry,
And lose the name of action.

    —HAMLET, PRINCE OF DENMARK

But, what we do determine oft we break.
Purpose is but the slave to memory;
Of violent birth, but poor validity:
Which now, like fruit unripe, sticks on the tree:
But fall, unshaken, when they mellow be.
Most necessary 't is, that we forget
To pay ourselves what to ourselves is debt;
What to ourselves in passion we propose,
The passion ending doth the purpose lose.
The violence of either grief or joy
Their own enactures with themselves destroy;
Where joy most revels grief doth most lament,
Grief joys, joy grieves, on slender accident.
This world is not for aye, nor 't is not strange
That even our loves should with our fortunes change;
For 't is a question left us yet to prove
Whether love lead fortune or else fortune love.
The great man down, you mark his favorite flies;
The poor advanc'd makes friends of enemies.
And hitherto doth love on fortune tend,
For who not needs shall never lack a friend;
And who in want a hollow friend doth try
Directly seasons him his enemy.
But, orderly to end where I begun,
Our wills and fates do so contrary run
That our devices still are overthrown,
Our thoughts are ours, their ends none of our own.

—HAMLET, PRINCE OF DENMARK

IMMORTALITY

In the corrupted currents of this world,
Offence's gilded hand may shove by justice;
And oft, 't is seen, the wicked prize itself
Buys out the law: But 't is not so above:
There is no shuffling, there the action lies
In his true nature; and we ourselves compell'd,
Even to the teeth and forehead of our faults,
To give in evidence.

—HAMLET, PRINCE OF DENMARK

SLANDER

Whose edge is sharper than the sword; whose tongue
Outvenoms all the worms of Nile; whose breath
Rides on the posting winds, and doth belie
All corners of the world,—kings, queens, and states,
Maids, matrons,—nay, the secrets of the grave
This viperous slander enters.—

—CYMBELINE

A GOOD NAME

Good name in man and woman, dear my lord,
Is the immediate jewel of their souls:
Who steals my purse steals trash; 'tis something,
   nothing;

'Twas mine, 'tis his, and has been slave to thousands;
But he that filches from me my good name,
Robs me of that which not enriches him,
And makes me poor indeed.

—OTHELLO

✑

FLATTERY

Like madness is the glory of this life,
As this pomp shows to a little oil and root.
We make ourselves fools to disport ourselves,
And spend our flatteries, to drink those men,
Upon whose age we void it up again,
With poisonous spite and envy.
Who lives that's not depraved, or depraves?
Who dies, that bears not one spurn to their graves
Of their friends' gift?
I should fear those that dance before me now,
Would one day stamp upon me: It has been done:
Men shut their doors against a setting sun.

—TIMON OF ATHENS

✑

GOLD

Gold? yellow, glittering, precious gold?
No, gods, I am no idle votarist.
Roots, you clear heavens! Thus much of this, will make
Black, white; foul, fair; wrong, right;

Base, noble; old, young; coward, valiant,
Ha, you gods! why this? What this, you gods? Why this
Will lug your priests and servants from your sides;
Pluck stout men's pillows from below their heads:

This yellow slave
Will knit and break religions; bless the accurs'd;
Make the hoar leprosy ador'd; place thieves,
And give them title, knee, and approbation,
With senators on the bench: this is it,
That makes the wappen'd widow wed again.

—TIMON OF ATHENS

∽◎

LOVE

I love you more than word can wield the matter,
Dearer than eye-sight, space, and liberty;
Beyond what can be valued, rich or rare;
No less than life, with grace, health, beauty, honor:
As much as child e'er lov'd, or father found.
A love that makes breath poor, and speech unable;
Beyond all manner of so much I love you.

—KING LEAR

∽◎

TO-MORROW

To-morrow, and to-morrow, and to-morrow,
Creeps in this petty pace from day to day,

To the last syllable of recorded time;
And all our yesterdays have lighted fools
The way to dusty death. Out, Out, brief candle!
Life's but a walking shadow; a poor player,
That struts and frets his hour upon the stage,
And then is heard no more: it is a tale
Told by an idiot, full of sound and fury,
Signifying nothing.

—Macbeth

HAVING DONE AND DOING

Time hath, my lord, a wallet at his back,
Wherein he puts alms for oblivion,
A great-sized monster of ingratitudes:
Those scraps are good deeds past; which are devour'd
As fast as they are made, forgot as soon
As done: Perseverance, dear my lord,
Keeps honor bright: to have done, is to hang
Quite out of fashion, like a rusty mail
In monumental mockery.

    Take the instant way;
For honor travels in a strait so narrow,
Where one but goes abreast; keep then the path;
For emulation hath a thousand sons,
That one by one pursue: if you give way,
Or hedge aside from the direct forthright,
Like to an enter'd tide, they all rush by,

And leave you hindmost;—
Or, like a gallant horse fallen in first rank,
Lie there for pavement to the abject rear,
O'errun and trampled on:

                Then what they do in present,
Though less than yours in past, must o'ertop yours:
For time is like a fashionable host,
That slightly shakes his parting guest by the hand;
And with his arms outstretch'd, as he would fly,
Grasps in the comer: welcome ever smiles,
And farewell goes out sighing. O! let not virtue seek
Remuneration for the thing it was; for beauty, wit,
High birth, vigor or bone, desert in service,
Love, friendship, charity, are subjects all
To envious and calumniating time.

One touch of nature makes the whole world kin,—
That all, with one consent, praise new-born gawds,
Though they are made and moulded of things past;
And give to dust, that is a little gilt,
More laud than gilt o'er-dusted.
The present eye praises the present object:
Since things in motion sooner catch the eye,
Than what not stirs.

                  —TROILUS AND CRESSIDA

FAVOR

　　　　　He that depends
Upon your favor swims with fins of lead,
And hews down oaks with rushes.

—C<small>ORIOLANUS</small>

POWER

Now we have shown our power,
Let us seem humbler after it is done,
Than when it was a doing.

—C<small>ORIOLANUS</small>

OPPORTUNITY

There is a tide in the affairs of men,
Which, taken at the flood, leads on to fortune;
Omitted, all the voyage of their life
Is bound in shallows and in miseries
On such a full sea are we now afloat;
And we must take the current when it serves,
Or lose our ventures.

—J<small>ULIUS</small> C<small>ÆSAR</small>

AMBITION'S LADDER

　　　But 't is a common proof
That lowliness is young ambition's ladder,

Whereto the climber-upward turns his face:
But when he once attains the upmost round,
He then unto the ladder turns his back,
Looks in the clouds, scorning the base degrees
By which he did ascend:

—Julius Cæsar

PRAYERS

We, ignorant of ourselves,
Beg often our own harms, which the wise powers
Deny us for our good; so find we profit,
By losing of our prayers.

I see, men's judgments are
A parcel of their fortunes; and things outward
Do draw the inward quality after them,
To suffer all alike.

When we in our viciousness grow hard,
(O misery on 't) the wise gods seal our eyes
In our own filth; drop our clear judgments; make us
Adore our errors; laugh at us, while we strut
To our confusion.

—Antony and Cleopatra

JEALOUSY

For where Love reigns, disturbing Jealousy
Doth call himself Affection's sentinel;
Gives false alarms, suggesteth mutiny,
And in a peaceful hour doth cry, "kill, kill;"
    Distempering gentle Love in his desire,
    As air and water do abate the fire.

This sour informer, this bate-breeding spy,
This canker that eats up love's tender spring,
This carry-tale, dissentious jealousy,
That sometime true news, sometime false doth bring.

              —Venus and Adonis

The aim of all is but to nurse the life
With honor, wealth, and ease, in waning age;
And in this aim there is such thwarting strife,
That one for all, or all for one we gage;
As life for honor in fell battles' rage;
Honor for wealth; and oft that wealth doth cost.
The death of all, and all together lost.
So that in vent'ring ill we leave to be
The things we are, for that which we expect;
And this ambitious foul infirmity,
In having much, torments us with defect
Of that we have: so then we do neglect

The thing we have, and, all for want of wit,
Make something nothing, by augmenting it.

—THE RAPE OF LUCRECE

⌒๏⌒

LOVE

Let me not to the marriage of true minds
Admit impediments. Love is not love
Which alters when it alteration finds,
Or bends with the remover to remove:
O no; it is an ever-fixed mark,
That looks on tempests, and is never shaken;
It is the star to every wandering bark,
Whose worth's unknown, although his height be
    taken.
Love's not Time's fool, though rosy lips and cheeks
Within his bending sickle's compass come;
Love alters not with his brief hours and weeks,
But bears it out even to the edge of doom.
If this be error, and upon me prov'd,
I never wirt, nor no man ever lov'd.

—SONNETS

⌒๏⌒

LOVE

Love's arms are peace, 'gainst rule, 'gainst sense,
   'gainst shame,

And sweetens, in the suffering pangs it bears,
The aloes of all forces, shocks, and fears.

—A Lover's Complaint

⌒⌒

BEAUTY IS BUT VAIN

Beauty is but a vain and doubtful good,
A shining gloss, that vadeth suddenly;
A flower that dies, when first it 'gins to bud;
A brittle glass, that's broken presently:
A doubtful good, a gloss, a glass, a flower,
Lost, vaded, broken, dead within an hour.

And as goods lost are seld or never found,
As vaded gloss no rubbing will refresh,
As flowers dead lie wither'd on the ground,
As broken glass no cement can redress,
So beauty, blemish'd once, for ever's lost,
In spite of physic, painting, pain, and cost.

—The Passionate Pilgrim

⌒⌒

A REAL MAN

His words are bonds, his oaths are oracles;
His love sincere, his thoughts immaculate;
His tears, pure messengers sent from his heart;
His heart as far from fraud as heaven from earth.

—The Two Gentlemen of Verona

WOMAN

Why, man, she is mine own;
And I as rich in having such a jewel,
As twenty seas, if all their sand were pearl,
The water nectar, and the rocks pure gold.

—THE TWO GENTLEMEN OF VERONA

LOVE

And, when love speaks, the voice of all the gods
Makes heaven drowsy with the harmony.

—LOVE'S LABOR'S LOST

BEAUTY

My beauty, though but mean,
Needs not the painted flourish of your praise;
Beauty is bought by judgment of the eye,
Not utter'd by base sale of seller's tongues.

—LOVE'S LABOR'S LOST

Better a little chiding than a great deal of heart-breaking.
Better three hours too soon than a minute too late.

—THE MERRY WIVES OF WINDSOR

MAN IS ONLY A DROP OF WATER

I to the world am like a drop of water,
That in the ocean seeks another drop;
Who, falling there to find his fellow forth,
Unseen, inquisitive, confounds himself.

—THE COMEDY OF ERRORS

No profit grows where is no pleasure ta'en;—
In brief, sir, study what you most affect.

—THE TAMING OF THE SHREW

LOVE

Things base and vile, holding no quantity
Love can transpose to form and dignity.
Love looks not with the eyes, but with the mind;
And therefore is wing'd Cupid painted blind.

—A MIDSUMMER NIGHT'S DREAM

MERCY

The quality of mercy is not strain'd;
It droppeth as the gentle rain from heaven
Upon the place beneath: It is twice bless'd;
It blesseth him that gives, and him that takes;

'Tis mightiest in the mightiest: it becomes
The throned monarch better than his crown;
His scepter shows the force of temporal power,
The attribute to awe and majesty,
Wherein doth sit the dread and fear of kings;
But mercy is above this sceptered sway,
It is enthroned in the hearts of kings,
It is an attribute to God himself;
And earthly power doth then show likest God's
When mercy seasons justice.
Though justice be thy plea, consider this—
That in the course of justice, none of us
Should see salvation: we do pray for mercy:
And that same prayer doth teach us all to render
The deeds of mercy.

—THE MERCHANT OF VENICE

VIRGINITY

It is not politic in the commonwealth of nature
to preserve virginity. Loss of virginity is rational
increase; and there was never virgin got till virginity
was first lost. That you were made of is metal to make
virgins. Virginity, by being once lost, may be ten times
found; by being ever kept, it is ever lost; 't is too cold a
companion; away with it . . .

There's little can be said in 't; 't is against the rule of
nature. To speak on the part of virginity is to accuse

your mothers; which is most infallible disobedience. He that hangs himself is a virgin; virginity murders itself; and should be buried in highways, out of all sanctified limit, as a desperate offendress against nature. Virginity breeds mites, much like a cheese; consumes itself to the very paring, and so dies with feeding his own stomach. Besides, virginity is peevish, proud, idle, made of self-love, which is the most inhibited sin in the canon. Keep it not; you cannot choose but lose by 't: Out with 't: within ten years it will make itself two, which is a goodly increase; and the principle itself not much the worse: Away with 't.

—All's Well That Ends Well

FRIENDSHIP IS NOT CONSTANT IN LOVE

Friendship is constant in all other things,
Save in the office and affairs of love:
Therefore, all hearts in love use their own tongues;
Let every eye negotiate for itself,
And trust no agent: for beauty is a witch,
Against whose charms faith melteth into blood.

—Much Ado About Nothing

INGRATITUDE

I hate ingratitude more in a man
Than lying, vainness, babbling, drunkenness,
Or any taint of vice, whose strong corruption
Inhabits our frail blood.

—TWELFTH NIGHT; OR, WHAT YOU WILL

ALL THE WORLD'S A STAGE

All the world's a stage,
And all the men and women merely players:
They have their exits, and their entrances;
And one man in his time plays many parts,
His acts being seven ages. At first, the infant,
Mewling and puking in the nurse's arms;
Then the whining schoolboy, with his satchel,
And shining morning face, creeping like a snail
Unwillingly to school: and then, the lover,
Sighing like a furnace, with a woeful ballad
Made to his mistress' eyebrow: Then, a soldier;
Full of strange oaths, and bearded like a pard,
Jealous in honor, sudden and quick in quarrel,
Seeking the bubble reputation
Even in the cannon's mouth: and then, the justice;
In fair round belly, with good capon lin'd,
With eyes severe, and beard of formal cut,
Full of wise saws and modern instances,
And so he plays his part: The sixth age shifts
In to the lean and slipper'd pantaloon;

With spectacles on nose, and pouch on side;
His youthful hose well sav'd, a world too wide
For his shrunk shank; and his big manly voice,
Turning again toward childish treble, pipes
And whistles, in his sound: Last scene of all,
That ends this strange eventful history,
Is second childishness, and more oblivion;
Sans teeth, sans eyes, sans taste, sans every thing.

—As You Like It

A JUST MAN

His life is parallel'd
Even with the stroke and line of his great justice;
He doth with holy abstinence subdue
That in himself, which he spurs on his power
To qualify in others: were he meal'd
With that which he corrects, then were he tyrannous;
But this being so, he's just.

—Measure for Measure

CHANGED COMPLEXIONS

Your chang'd complexions are to me a mirror,
Which shows me mine chang'd too: for I must be
A party in this alteration, finding
Myself thus alter'd with it.

—The Winter's Tale

We are such stuff as dreams are made on, and our
    little life is rounded with a sleep.

—THE TEMPEST

WOMAN

But she as far surpasseth woman,
As greatest does least.

— THE TEMPEST

PAINTING THE LILY

Therefore, to be possess'd with double pomp,
To guard a title that was rich before,
To gild refined gold, to paint the lily,
To throw a perfume on the violet,
To smooth the ice, or add another hue
Unto the rainbow, or with taper-light
To seek the beauteous eye of heaven to garnish,
Is wasteful and ridiculous excess.

—KING JOHN

SPOTLESS REPUTATION

My dear, dear lord,
The purest treasure mortal times afford,

Is spotless reputation; that away,
Men are but gilded loam, or painted clay.
A jewel in a ten-times-barr'd-up chest
Is a bold spirit in a loyal breast,
Mine honor is my life; both grow in one;
Take honor from me, and my life is done:
Then, dear my liege, mine honor let me try;
In that I live, and for that will I die.

—KING RICHARD II

He gave you all the duties of a man;
Trimm'd up your praises with a princely tongue;
Spoke your deservings like a chronicle;
Making you ever better than his praise.

—KING HENRY IV, PART I

GOLD

How quickly nature falls into revolt
When gold becomes her object!
For this the foolish over-careful fathers
Have broke their sleep with thoughts, their brains
    with care,
Their bones with industry;
For this they have engrossed and pil'd up
The canker'd heaps of strange-achieved gold
For this they have been thoughtful to invest

Their sons with arts, and martial exercises:
When, like the bee, culling from every flower
The virtuous sweets;
Our thighs pack'd with wax, our mouths with honey,
We bring it to the hive; and, like the bees.
Are murder'd for our pain. This bitter taste
Yields his engrossments to the ending father.

—KING HENRY IV, PART II

COMMONWEALTH OF BEES

Therefore doth heaven divide
The state of man in divers functions,
Setting endeavour in continual motion;
To which is fixed, as an aim or butt,
Obedience: for so work the honey bees;
Creatures, that, by a rule in nature, teach
The act of order to a peopled kingdom.
They have a king, and officers of sorts:
Where some, like magistrates, correct at home;
Others, like merchants, venture trade abroad;
Others, like soldiers, armed in their stings,
Make boot upon the summer's velvet buds;
Which pillage they with merry march bring home
To the tent-royal of their emperor:
Who, busied in his majesty, surveys
The singing masons building roofs of gold;
The civil citizens kneading up the honey;
The poor mechanic porters crowding in
Their heavy burthens at his narrow gate;

The sad-ey'd justice, with his surly hum,
Delivering o'er to executors pale
The lazy yawning drone.

         I this infer,—
That many things, having full reference
To one concent, may work contrariously;
As many arrows, loosed several ways,
Come to one mark; as many ways meet in one town;
As many fresh streams meet in one salt sea;
As many lines close in the dial's center;
So many thousand actions, once afoot,
End in one purpose, and be all well borne
Without defeat.

                 —King Henry V

GLORY

Glory is like a circle in the water,
Which never ceaseth to enlarge itself.
Till, by broad spreading, it disperse to nought

                 —King Henry VI, Part I

CARE

Care is no cure, but rather corrosive,
For things that are not to be remedied.

                 —King Henry VI, Part I

TRUTH

What stronger breastplate than a heart untainted!
Thrice is he arm'd that hath his quarrel just;
And he but naked, though lock'd up in steel,
Whose conscience with injustice is corrupted.

—KING HENRY VI, PART II

A little gale will soon disperse that cloud,
And blow it to the source from whence it came:
Thy very beams will dry those vapours up;
For every cloud engenders not a storm.

—KING HENRY VI, PART III

MY CROWN IS IN MY HEART

My crown is in my heart, not on my head;
Not deck'd with diamonds and Indian stones,
Nor to be seen: my crown is call'd content;
A crown it is that seldom kings enjoy.

—KING HENRY VI, PART III

CONSCIENCE

I'll not meddle with it, (it is a dangerous thing,)
it makes a man a coward; a man cannot steal but it

accuseth him; a man cannot swear but it checks him; a man cannot lie with his neighbor's wife but it detects him: 'T is a blushing shame-faced spirit that mutinies in a man's bosom; it fills one full of obstacles; it made me once restore a purse of gold that by chance I found; it beggars any man that keeps it: it is turned out of towns and cities for a dangerous thing; and every man that means to live well endeavors to trust to himself, and live without it.

—KING RICHARD III

THE STATE OF MAN

This is the state of man: Today he puts forth
The tender leaves of hopes, tomorrow blossoms,
And bears his blushing honors thick upon him:
The third day comes a frost, a killing frost:
And,—when he thinks, good easy man, full surely
His greatness is a ripening,—nips his root,
And then he falls, as I do, I have ventur'd,
Like little wanton boys that swim on bladders,
This many summers in a sea of glory;
But far beyond my depth: my high-blown pride
At length broke under me; and now has left me,
Weary, and old with service, to the mercy
Of a rude stream, that must forever hide me.
Vain pomp and glory of this world, I hate ye;
I feel my heart new open'd: O, how wretched
Is that poor man that hangs on princes' favors!

There is, betwixt that smile we would aspire to,
That sweet aspect of princes, and their ruin,
More pangs and fears than wars or women have;
And when he falls, he falls like Lucifer,
Never to hope again.

—KING HENRY VIII

THE TOMB

Secure from worldly chances and mishaps:
Here lurks no treason, here no envy swells,
Here grow no damned grudges; here are no storms,
No noise, but silence and eternal sleep.
In peace and honor rest you here.

—TITUS ANDRONICUS

FLATTERY

For flattery is the bellows blows up sin;
The thing the which is flatter'd, but a spark,
To which that blast gives heat and stronger glowing.

—PERICLES

THE ROSE

Of all flowers, methinks a rose is best.

It is the very emblem of a maid:
For when the west wind courts her gently,
How modestly she blows, and paints the sun
With her chaste blushes! when the north comes near
    her,
Rude and impatient, then, like chastity,
She locks her beauties in her bud again,
And leaves him to base briers.

—The Two Noble Kinsmen

He needs no cunning that for truth doth fight.

Unkindness strikes a deeper wound than steel.

—A Yorkshire Tragedy